DRIVE OF A LIFETIME

THE AUTOBIOGRAPHY

JAMIE WHINCUP

DRIVE OF A LIFETIME

THE AUTOBIOGRAPHY

WITH SCOTT GULLAN

PENGUIN BOOKS

UK | USA | Canada | Ireland | Australia
India | New Zealand | South Africa | China

Penguin Books is part of the Penguin Random House group of companies whose addresses can be found at global.penguinrandomhouse.com

First published by Penguin Books in 2021

Front and back cover photographs by Daniel Kalisz/Getty Images

Cover design by Alex Ross © Penguin Random House Australia Pty Ltd
Internal design and typesetting by Midland Typesetters, Australia
Typeset in 12.5/18 pt Minion Pro

Printed and bound in Australia by Griffin Press, part of Ovato, an accredited ISO AS/NZS 14001 Environmental Management Systems printer

A catalogue record for this book is available from the National Library of Australia

ISBN 978 1 76104 488 5

penguin.com.au

This book is dedicated to
the next generation

CONTENTS

1

GENETICS V. DEVELOPMENT

ARE you born to be something, or is it your childhood that shapes who you become?

It's a question I often find myself contemplating. Was there something in my DNA that meant I was going to become a racecar driver?

If you're a basketballer it's a massive advantage to be tall and there are plenty of sports where genetics play a big part, but in motor racing is there a special characteristic that's required?

It has been put to me that you need a brain that isn't scared, one that doesn't react to a dangerous situation in a normal manner.

I recently watched a documentary on American climber Alex Honnold called *Free Solo*, which shows how he climbs rock faces without a harness. It's crazy stuff and they did an interesting exercise where they tested the reactions of his brain to certain scenarios.

Dramatic events such as car crashes, trains derailing and people being badly injured are shown to him – and his brain doesn't react to the danger. The consensus is that he doesn't experience fear like the rest of us.

I can see a link with being a Supercar driver, as we have different reactions to dangerous situations compared to the normal person. When cars are spinning out and crashing in front of you, I'm not getting frightened – I'm trying to pick the best way out of it.

How your brain is wired in regards to dangerous situations and its ability to cope with long periods of sustained concentration does fall on the genetic side. But I still put a lot of emphasis on what you do growing up and the development you have at an early age.

So, did my father having me sit on his lap as he drove the boat, or as he took the motorbike for a spin around the block, play a part in my motorsport pursuit? Or the fact he let me drive the tractor and the ride-on mower, even when I could hardly reach the pedals?

It probably all played a part, and I'm a believer that what you do in your younger years up to the age of 14 really shapes you as a person.

The example that is set by your parents when you're growing up and going through puberty can go a long way to determining who you become.

Maybe I'm genetically suited to something else but have never actually discovered it.

What I do know is that I was seven years old when my father took me over to my Uncle Graeme's for a visit that set me on my path.

*

'Have a seat in that, mate.'

I was staring at this beautiful striking red go-kart that was parked inside my Uncle Graeme's garage.

The shock of what I was staring at was still sinking in as I lowered myself into the seat.

'How do you like it?' my father, David, asked.

I looked up at him and then across to my uncle, who was smiling. But his smile wasn't as big as mine.

'It's pretty good.'

I'd never really expressed any desire to get a go-kart but as I sat there with my hands gripping the steering wheel, I knew this was now going to be my sport. Although my first attempt didn't suggest I had much of a future in it.

The next day Dad, Graeme and I went up to the Eastern Lions Kart Club at Whittlesea, a northern suburb of Melbourne, a 30-minute drive from where we lived in Greensborough.

I had no idea what I was doing and it showed. I was useless.

While they didn't say anything, I could sense there was some concern in the camp as I battled to get the kart past idle for the entire afternoon.

I spluttered around the tiny circuit like a pensioner on a scooter, only slower. But the next week I went back, then the weekend after that. For 12 months Whittlesea was my home away from home as I learnt to become a go-karter.

Something I didn't realise at the time was that Dad was having to change the spark plug after each run. It was dead because so much oil was getting on it, which was caused by how slowly I was going.

I was only eight years old so Dad wanted me to just practise before we started racing.

After my inglorious beginning, I'd quickly got the hang of the machinery and was soon hurling myself around the circuit, which was around 300m, as fast as possible.

Dad had set a lap time of around the 15-second mark at Whittlesea which I had to achieve before he would let me race at other tracks.

I eventually got it consistently, so in 1992 my racing career officially began in the rookies class – age group 7 to 12 – and I had a helmet that was almost bigger than my body.

My first venture away from Whittlesea was to a track at Brooklyn, just near the West Gate Bridge – different from the track you see today though. It blew my mind – it was massive, almost double the size of my home circuit. I felt like I was getting lost driving around it because it was that long.

It took me a year to win my first trophy and that wasn't even for getting on the podium – it was an encouragement award for coming fourth. My first real trophy came not long after that when I finished second at Swan Hill.

The last Sunday of every month was club championship day. Points were collated from each club day to decide who was the champion at the end of the season.

There were usually between 10 and 15 kids racing and I improved quickly as the year progressed, finishing second in the championship.

That's when I got my first insight into the cut-throat competitive nature of motorsport.

It turned out the kid who'd won got penalised; his father

had been using special fuel to gain an advantage. The trophy was now mine, and the first of many I'd hoped, as I was loving my new pursuit.

It was no surprise, really, given I'd grown up around motorsport.

My dad and Graeme had been involved for much of their lives, although initially they raced speedboats together.

Then Graeme got into racecar driving throughout the 1980s in a red Chevrolet Monza. His cars were always red (when he had the choice), which was why my first go-kart had been that colour. He'd also spent time working with touring car legend Allan Moffat as part of his team.

I'd heard many stories about his time with Moffat, who won four touring car championships as well as Australia's biggest race, the Bathurst 1000, four times.

As a young kid I'd often tag along in the big truck they used to transport the car when Graeme was racing, usually to Sandown, which was the main racetrack in Melbourne.

My mother, Sandra, was happy when I took a liking to the sport instead of following one of dad's other passions – pistol shooting. While they were both dangerous pursuits, she thought the go-karts were the least dangerous so therefore it was encouraged.

The other member of our family, Sally, five years older than me, was too busy with calisthenics (a type of gymnastic exercise) to take too much notice about the increasing number of trophies her brother was bringing home.

My first couple of years in rookies had gone well and by my third season things had got a lot more serious. We were racing all around the state; wherever there was a race we'd be there. From up the bush in Numurkah to down the highway to Geelong or all the way up to Mildura.

There was even the odd race interstate. In 1994, the year I turned 11, I won the Adelaide Formula 1 Grand Prix Kart race and also snared the NSW rookie state championships to go with my Victorian title.

The following year I had 25 starts for 19 wins, three second places and one third. That earnt me Rookie of the Year status for the second time. Karting had gone from an interest to a full-time passion and, the more I did it, the better I was becoming.

To be honest, nothing else interested me. I would have a kick of the football at lunchtime at Eltham College but that was about it. School wasn't really my thing and my routine during the week would be to get home as soon as I could, grab something to eat and then head to the garage to tinker with the kart.

After every race the whole thing had to be taken apart and given a good clean and service. A day at a go-kart track was like living in a dust bowl, so usually there was dirt and mud clinging to everything.

Wheels, tyres, sprockets, the engine . . . they all came off. If stickers had been damaged, they would be replaced. 'It doesn't cost any money to look good,' was Dad's motto.

He was adamant you had to make sure every tiny little thing was maintained and ready to go. The key was not to get lazy.

A dirty kart wasn't a slow kart, but if it was dirty it was obvious that you hadn't checked everything.

More often than not it was during the cleaning process that problems were found. For example, a crack in the chassis would often be discovered under a couple of layers of dirt.

Dad's attitude soon rubbed off on me, and cleaning is still part of my routine today. Before every Supercars race I always clean my helmet. It's my ritual, even if it doesn't look dirty. It has also become a safety check to make sure the radio and air vents are working.

This habit had served me well from day one and was important as I took the next step into the junior ranks.

It was a daunting move in a way, because I was a 12-year-old battling kids up to the age of 15. And it was full-on. We started racing 40 weekends a year all around Australia.

It's fair to say I didn't see many Fridays at Eltham College. Dad and I would often hit the road on a Thursday night if, for example, it was a competition at Swan Hill, which was a four-hour drive away.

On Friday we'd go to the track and practise all day, which would involve four or five sessions to dial in the kart. There would be anywhere between 200 and 300 entries at each race meeting.

On Saturday there would be qualifying followed by a couple of 30-lap races, which would usually take around half an hour.

The Sunday would involve a pre-final race and then a final of up to 40 laps. By the time the presentations were done it would be 6pm before we'd get in the car and start the journey home. A hamburger somewhere on the road would be dinner and then I'd inevitably sleep most of the way.

The trailer would be put in the garage, I'd go straight to bed and then wake up in the morning and head off to school.

That was our routine and it obviously needed some dedicated parents and a supportive uncle . . . luckily, I had three of the best.

Data logging, Italian factories, Whincup Racing Team. Welcome to the world of a 13-year-old junior go-karter.

We'd made the big call to change brands of go-karts. All through rookies and the start of juniors I'd used an Arrow kart made by famous Australian manufacturer Drew Price Engineering.

But now the Whincup Racing Team – my uncle Graeme had started it when he was competing and we were now resurrecting it – was being backed by Italian brand CRG. They'd supplied us with the latest CRG piston port kart, two engines and a dedicated mechanic at the major events.

I'd learnt there was so much more to karting than just getting in and going flat knacker.

Our kart now had an on-board data logger, so after each practice session I was able to download data and look at exactly what was happening out there.

For the 1997 season we also stepped up to a new sprint kart series called FMK. It was regarded as the best in the country because it was set up along international lines.

Most countries in the world used the same classes. I was moving into the Junior Intercontinental A, which was limited to drivers under 16. After that there were the senior classes,

Intercontinental A and Formula A, which was the top of the tree in Australian karting.

We were hit and miss in our first FMK season and finished third behind Michael Caruso from NSW. He'd dominated and we were starting to have serious concerns about our European kart. We simply didn't have the pace, and became fascinated by anything Caruso did as we tried to figure out why he was so fast.

At one stage he ran a piece of tape along the middle of his axle – and we spent hours sussing out what it was doing. It was a great tactic for him, because in the end we used all of our time worrying about somebody else and not concentrating on making ourselves go faster.

I'm certain he was just doing it to put everyone off. It was a lesson learnt that I still refer back to today because those tactics still go on.

The competition was getting fierce and one of my main opponents had become one of my best friends.

Will Davison came from a motor racing family and had also started his karting career at the Eastern Lions Kart Club in Whittlesea. His father, Richard, was an Australian Formula 2 champion while his older brother, Alex, had progressed from karts to Formula Ford racing.

We were both on the same path and, despite being at each other's throats on the track, we enjoyed hanging out away from it.

That wasn't the case with my other main rival, who I didn't really know too much about. He hailed from Sydney and his name was Mark Winterbottom.

*

'We need to cut back on a few things.'

Dad was addressing the family, who were seated around the dinner table. Our financial position was the subject being discussed.

Racing go-karts around the country was an expensive business and Dad was feeling the pinch.

'We need to think of ways to save money,' he said. 'Take shampoo, for example. There's no need to use more than what would cover a twenty-cent piece.'

My sister seemed bemused at the suggestion while my mother just nodded.

She'd been dealing with the situation for some time and had even gotten to the point where she was too embarrassed to invite friends over because of the state of the couch in the living room.

It had the wood poking through the fabric but there was no money for furniture in the budget; every spare cent was being poured into go-karts.

At various times Dad had worked three jobs. His main job had been in a printing press before he actually bought his own. He'd never had any specific qualifications but was the sort of person who relied on common sense and just getting out there and having a crack.

If he was building something – which he often was, given our shed was full of tools – and he didn't have the skills or the knowledge to do it, then he'd go and find someone who did and learn it from them. He was a very determined person, and my uncle used to always joke that if you wanted something done all you had to say was: 'Dave, I don't reckon you could do it.' And the next minute he would find a way to do it.

Dad was all go and no show. He didn't really care what anyone thought as long as he was getting the job sorted. Graeme, on the other hand, while he had plenty of go he also loved the show. He was the youngest of the three Whincup brothers – my uncle Allan was the oldest – and was the entrepreneur, running a T-shirt printing business in Preston whilst dabbling in the life of a racecar driver.

They were a fair bit different, but tight as tight.

Mum had a completely different personality to both of them. She was quiet, conservative and had worked as a dressmaker in the city for years before becoming a full-time stay-at-home mother. She got things done with a minimum of fuss.

I'd get home from school and dump my clothes in a pile on the floor as I rushed to get down to the garage. Without fail, by the time I returned those clothes had disappeared and would be washed, ironed and back in my wardrobe by the end of the week.

Mum was a calming influence in the crazy world of karting that we were all living 24/7.

And it was about to get crazier.

For the 1998 season, when I was 15, Dad agreed it was time to move into the senior ranks. I'd shown I could handle racing kids who were two or three years older, but now some of my rivals were going to be double my age!

To make the transition we again changed karts to another Italian brand, Tecno, through an importer based out of

Horsham, in western Victoria, called Remo Luciani. Remo imported everything for the kart from the chains and sprockets to the Parilla engine. He became our go-to person.

We also hired a mechanic for the first time, Peter 'Topsi' Temopoulos, who would be there on race days, tuning the kart, getting the tyre pressure right and making sure everything was ticking over.

Dad and Graeme had managed to do it previously, but to take the next step we needed to get professionals involved. Topsi was a friend of Remo's and quickly became an integral part of our team. His influence was substantial, and I wouldn't have been as successful or have developed so quickly without him.

We were certainly the most professional-looking outfit thanks to my uncle's black and yellow Whincup Racing Team button-up shirts, which he'd produced for our senior debut. They had Remo Racing plastered on the back, and every time we arrived at a meeting we'd be dressed as a team in black trousers and these shirts.

We had our own tent set up on the side of the track with all the gear in it. Everything was clean, tidy and organised. People were even calling us the Holden Dealer Team of go-kart racing. Clearly, from the outside, we looked to have a pretty schmick operation.

It's funny how much looks can be deceiving, because like many others we were operating on less than we needed. This was obvious at the Australian Kart Championship.

In the carby tuning session the morning before the finals, it was raining heavily and I was running with Dunlops, but the Bridgestones were a far better wet weather tyre and what I thought I needed to win.

But Dad wouldn't budge. He simply didn't have the money to buy the new tyres. 'I'll use the money from my coin jar,' I pleaded. No go, so out I went with the Dunlops.

Fortunately for us, we got lucky with the track drying out more than we all expected for the pre-final, and the Dunlops ended up being the faster tyres, carrying us to a memorable victory.

There were a few more of those good moments throughout the season as the transition into the big time went smoother than we could have ever imagined.

On top of being the Australian Intercontinental A champion I also won the state titles for that class in Victoria, NSW and South Australia.

There was a lot of debate about what I should do next. There was one school of thought that I would benefit from another year in Intercontinental A. I didn't agree and, thankfully, nor did our team manager.

'We're going to Formula A,' Dad said.

A second place in the opening event of 1999 justified the decision. I'd actually led the final before being passed mid-race, which annoyed me immensely.

There were no kid gloves from Dad or my uncle when I didn't get the results we expected. We were all striving for excellence and, if I didn't do my job, the team suffered. This was rammed home to me repeatedly.

'Get your head on,' would be my uncle's words before each race.

He would say it just as I'd got into my seat and was strapped in, ready to go. Graeme would tap the side of his head and then point at me.

It was my signal to lock in. It worked.

I had no idea what I was walking into.

We'd just pulled up at Uncle Graeme's house because Dad had told me that's where we were having dinner. But we didn't go straight inside. Instead, he led me to the adjoining factory.

Graeme was waiting for us but I didn't see him – all I saw was the Formula Ford racecar that was parked inside. I was stunned.

It was déjà vu. Eight years earlier I'd walked into the same garage and been surprised to find a brand-new go-kart. It was happening all over again, and I couldn't take my eyes off this shiny red racecar.

This was the next stepping stone from karting to the single-seater, open-wheel formula racing, which was regarded around the world as the breeding ground for future F1 drivers. But I had literally never given Formula Ford one single thought.

I was a go-kart racer and I'd figured that was what I was going to do for the rest of my life.

'All right, we're racing Formula Ford now. OK,' was my response when I was able to get some words out.

Then all sorts of questions popped into my head. Where did they get it from? How much did it cost? Could we afford to run a team in Formula Ford?

I didn't get many straight answers, as I think Dad didn't want his teenage son to be worried about such details. Later I found out that Graeme had invested significantly.

There were so many exciting parts to this amazing development in my life with the Formula Fords racing on all the big racetracks around the country, even at Bathurst. Sometimes the events were even held at the same time as an Australian Touring Car Championship round.

Before any of that could happen we still had some unfinished business in karts.

There was only one round of Formula A remaining at Eastern Creek in Sydney and I had a handy points lead in the championship after securing a couple of victories earlier in the season.

Dad made it clear that I couldn't take my eye off the prize and I got the impression that if I didn't win the Formula A title, then he was prepared to put my Formula Ford debut on ice for a year.

There was no way I was letting that happen. When I secured victory in the pre-final race the title was mine. Luckily I had enough points in the bank because I blew the engine in the final and didn't finish the race.

I'd now reached the pinnacle in go-karts in Australia and it felt right to take the next step.

The funny thing was I'd never visualised any of this because I hadn't been the sort of kid to look up to a hero. There were no posters on my wall of F1 superstars or touring car drivers and I'd never got an autograph in my life.

If I had been that way inclined there was an obvious candidate, a former Eastern Lions boy who'd made good and had just won his third Australian Touring Car Championship.

His name? Craig Lowndes.

2
PLAYING THE LONG GAME

THE long game is really hard. And it's getting harder. Everything now seems to be focused on instant reward, with people shying away from working on something for weeks, months and even years without getting a pay-off straight away.

It is really difficult to keep motivated and focused on the long game when you're getting no feedback and no reward whatsoever. It takes real dedication and mental strength to be able to sustain that.

I was taught by my parents that you worked hard, you saved your money and you got ready for retirement. You basically worked the first half of your life as hard as you possibly could to make the second part of your life as comfortable as can be.

But it's not just finances – the long-game principle can be applied to everything in life, like fitness or even deciding to have a drink. If you do a 20-minute workout and smash yourself with weights or do 100 push-ups in five minutes, that will get a good gain and you will feel bulky and great for going out that night. That is a classic example of the short game, whereas the long game in terms of fitness would be a program that makes you fit, healthy and able to live longer rather than just looking good for a night out.

I'm so aware and geared up about this long game. What I perceive as the short game stuff really annoys me, the whole get-rich-quick schemes and get-fit quick schemes. While I understand you have to stay relevant, fresh and adaptable, I get really nervous about fads and trends. Every time something new comes along I always ask the question, 'Is this going to be good for me long term or is it just a short-term fix?' And also 'Are people still going to be doing this in 100 years or will it die off?'

Luckily, I did play the long game when I got a call from a mystery Brisbane number 15 years ago.

'This isn't working and we think it's best if Jamie moves on.'

The principal of Eltham College was leaning forward in his chair and delivering the news. Even though I wasn't all that surprised to hear it, it still hit hard. And it hit harder on my father, who was seated next to me.

He felt disappointed that he'd done all he could to get me a good education at a private school and I'd blown it halfway through Year 11. The problem was I didn't see school as part of my long game. In fact, I hated school. I always had.

I'd been going to Eltham College, in the north-east of Melbourne, since kindergarten. All my schooling had been at the same place, I'd travelled along the same road, got off at the same place, gone into the same classrooms, played on the same ovals. I was just sick of it. But there was a lot more to my departure than just being sick of my surroundings.

As my go-kart career had started to take off I began cutting every Friday, and often Thursday as well, to travel around the country to compete. Understandably, this wasn't greatly received by my teachers.

It was obvious early on that I didn't get along well with authority. That certainly isn't the case later in life where I have massive respect for the police, government and the laws. But as I progressed through school, I lost respect for the teachers.

My outlook on school had got progressively worse as I caught the go-kart bug. The worst day of my life was the first day of school at the start of every year.

I would have just had the summer off, water skiing with family and friends up on the Murray River or just riding my bike around at home. I loved the freedom that came with school holidays.

The mere thought of having to go to that place again five days a week for a 10-week term just made me feel sick in the stomach. Often I would sit on the end of my bed crying and saying to my parents: 'Please don't make me go to school, please don't make me.'

Once I did get there I embraced it. Well, to a degree – I certainly wasn't sitting in the corner sulking. I had plenty of good friends there and I really enjoyed hanging out with them, having a kick of the footy at lunchtime like everyone else. But I was a square peg in a round hole.

The thing was, I loved freedom and my parents certainly allowed me to enjoy that. They made me make my own choices and I'm sure there were plenty of times where they could see I was going to make the wrong decision, but those times were valuable life lessons.

Sometimes you've just got to make your own mistakes to understand why that is the wrong way. It's almost like you know something is wrong but you want to trial it, and then you actually know it was wrong because you've lived through it. From there you can make the right choices, and I'm really grateful I was given a lot of freedom growing up.

I actually learnt how to drive at a fairly young age or, should I say, I learnt how to understand the controls of things and how they operated. Whether it was the car, our boat, a tractor or ride-on mower, Dad would let me sit on his lap and steer.

This was happening from the age of five, so naturally my confidence grew over the years and by the time I was a teenager I was more than ready to do some experimentation.

One day at Corowa, where we'd holidayed as a family since I was two years old, my friend Matty and I decided to take Dad's red truck for a spin. He'd bought this old Land-Cruiser, painted it and altered it so it could lower our boat in and out of the water – the ramp there was a tricky operation.

We'd decided to take the truck for a spin as our parents were out to lunch at a near-by winery with friends. There was this small area down near the boat ramp and we thought we'd go around this big tree and back up to the car park.

I was too small to handle all of the controls so I took charge of the pedals and steering wheel while my mate did the gears. We nailed it from the start and decided to do a few laps of the tree, much to the delight of some other interested parents.

We managed to get it back to its parking spot before my parents got home. We were convinced we'd got away with it. In hindsight I'm pretty sure we didn't, as the other parents would have definitely let slip. But no-one got hurt and nothing was damaged, so Mum and Dad decided to let it go.

My next borrowing of Dad's vehicle wasn't as successful.

This time I would have been around 15 when I decided to take Dad's Ford Falcon V8 station wagon to do some fishies up the dirt road near the caravan park. I started doing a few but then quickly struck trouble with the car spinning and sliding into this big drain on the side of the road.

It was a heavy impact but miraculously it hit perfectly sideways, which popped both tyres off the rim but somehow didn't damage the rim or bend the suspension. There was a house close-by where an elderly lady lived. She knew us because we sometimes stored our boat around the back, so I decided it was the perfect place to hide the damaged car.

She was hard of hearing, so I'm not sure she really knew what was going on. I frantically rang Matty, who came around, and we did a quick dash into the local service station, where we managed to somehow inflate the tyres and pop them back on the rim. We then dashed back to the house, and as I was putting the tyres back on I saw my parents arrive at the caravan park.

I knew I was cooked. I slowly, and as silently as I could, drove the station wagon back and parked it behind the family caravan. After a few long deep breaths I walked around the front, fully expecting a barrage of: 'Where the hell have you been? Where's the car? You're grounded for a week.'

Instead, I found my parents laughing.

When they asked where we'd been I quickly said just down the street and the conversation moved on. I couldn't believe I'd got away with it, although again I suspected my father knew more than he was letting on. Given that the car had been returned in working order (only just), he was more than happy to turn a blind eye.

'What do I do with this?'

The question wasn't actually directed at anyone. I was just making the point to myself about how different my new surroundings were in the Formula Ford car.

I was referring to the gearbox, as this was the first time I would be using one. There were no changes of gears required in karting and there were plenty of other differences too, including dealing with the suspension and shock absorbers, and the size of the tracks was on a whole new level.

Gone were the tight go-kart tracks, replaced by proper V8 circuits such as Bathurst. Talk about a steep learning curve.

But after 10 years karting, even though I still loved it and was still growing in it, having another huge challenge was exciting.

We ran our own team in year one and used Graeme's old truck from back in his sports sedan racing days. It needed a bit of a refurbishment and we gave it a modern makeover, including putting in a crane that was able to pick up the Formula Ford car and swing it onto the back of the truck.

A small kitchen and shower were installed while the three of us would sleep in a section at the top of the cabin, where there was a 3-by-2.5 metre flat mattress.

That's what I loved about Formula Ford: it was a real family affair, although we got some much-needed help from a few people in the know.

A good family friend, Ron Harrop, was a highly renowned engineer at the Holden Racing Team, and he helped us out with all the basic fundamentals for engineering a racecar. It was a critical component because while my father and uncle knew how to get the car to the track and how to run it, Ron was really good at being able to engineer the car to make it go faster.

Not that we went fast enough in 2000. I didn't win a race for the whole season competing in various state rounds, but I took away a lot of learnings about this whole new world I now lived in.

The following year we raced in the national series and I finished third behind my good mate Will 'Davo' Davison, who'd started in Formula Ford a year earlier than I had, and Will Power, who would go on years later to race IndyCar in the US.

It soon became obvious that to taste the ultimate success you had to be part of a professional team and in 2002 we joined Sonic Motorsport, which was run by Mick Ritter, whose brother Greg had won the 1999 championship and had helped us with our initial transition to the category.

I actually took over Davo's seat with the team and leased the car that he'd driven to win the championship the previous year.

Mick was an astounding bloke. He was quite rough on the outside and first impressions would put many off. A night wouldn't go by where a six-pack of beer wasn't consumed along with a packet of Winnie Blues. But he was an unbelievable teacher of young people. A number of Australia's top Supercar drivers have spent time with Mick, including myself, Davo and Dave Reynolds.

While he didn't have any children himself, he was like a father to us. He made sure we stayed grounded, had good morals and understood what motorsport was really about.

Mick was big on emphasising that sport wasn't all glitz and glamour, he made sure we understood what it took behind the scenes to get a car to the track, and how it was a team effort. He made sure that even though we drivers were the stars of the show, so to speak, we still served our time in the workshop like everyone else. We weren't allowed to just swan in for the test day, race day and a few debriefs. Mick made sure we were at the workshop working on the car, washing the tents, cleaning the trolleys and the truck.

That ensured we had a true understanding of the sport. I don't believe you can get the most out of yourself as an athlete without fully understanding everything that's required to pull it all together.

We understood how much time and effort had been put in to prepare the car, which meant we had more respect for the car. This way, we knew all the sacrifices and hard work the team had put in – and that made a huge difference.

The new car and team worked wonders. We won the opening race of the season and really never looked back, virtually wrapping up the championship with a round to go.

This created a dilemma on the home front.

The expenses of being in Formula Ford were steep, and towards the end of 2002 it was becoming obvious that we could no longer afford it. We'd managed to get a few sponsors, most of them were mainly family friends or associates, like the paper supplier to Dad's printing press, but the well had run dry.

Mum's oven was on the blink and she was getting more and more concerned about the state of the couch.

There was a perception that the natural stepping stone in motorsport for a young driver was to climb the ladder through karting to Formula Ford and then, with a Formula 1 drive as the ultimate goal, head off to Europe.

That was never going to happen for me. Getting the money just to even get a ticket to fly to Europe was going to be a stretch, let alone going over there to drive.

Like when I started karting, I thought once I got into Formula Ford I would just keep doing that, but for the first time doubt was starting to creep in. If I didn't find a way to become a professional driver in 2003, then my career was in strife.

*

It was like I was strapped to a rocket.

I was hurtling around the track at the Mallala Motorsport Park, an iconic venue 45 minutes north of Adelaide, in a Supercar. I had never driven a Supercar. In fact, I had never experienced anything like what was happening.

The horsepower of the engine was amazing, the acceleration was phenomenal. It would take off, and I'd just be hanging on looking for the brake marker to know when to pull up.

It was a small track, but there was a fast sweeper on the back straight and that was enough to feel the raw speed, which scared the hell out of me.

The whole thing was bizarre in so many ways as it was also the first time I'd driven behind a windscreen. All through karting and Formula Ford, if you needed airflow you just cracked your visor. Going this fast and not having the wind in your face was a quite unique weird feeling that was going to take some getting used to.

My first drive in a Supercar – it was an EL Ford Falcon – came about through friends of ours who knew Ross Halliday, a veteran driver and team owner.

He was happy to give me a chance and I was so pleased I managed to have a nice clean day. The most important thing was I didn't make a goose of myself, I didn't do anything stupid in what was a good introduction to what potentially could be my next calling.

This gave my uncle and father confidence to take the next step, and so they approached Garry Rogers, who owned Garry Rogers Motorsport (GRM). Garry supported Mick Ritter and Sonic Motorsport with money from Valvoline, which was the major sponsor of his Supercars and also supported us in Formula Ford.

Garry had been keeping tabs on my progress in Formula Ford and agreed to give me a test run in a Supercar at Winton, a tight track near Benalla in country Victoria. It bucketed down with rain on the morning of the test, so we waited a couple of hours until the track dried out before my audition began.

I was nervous and once again blown away by the power of the car. The H-pattern gearbox was causing me some problems and halfway through the day I was second guessing about whether I was cut out for Supercars. Everything felt so weird compared to the Formula Ford and I kept asking myself: 'Is this for me?'

While I didn't break any records, importantly I didn't do anything silly, with the only issue being I missed a few gear changes throughout the day and had some over-revs.

Despite my doubts I clearly passed the test, as Garry offered me my first drive in a Supercars race at the Queensland 500 in September. It was the perfect place to debut, as the Queensland Raceway in Ipswich is known as 'The Paper Clip' because it looks like a big paperclip and is nice and flat with plenty of run-off.

There was a minor curveball to this momentous occasion. I would also be competing in Formula Ford on the same weekend and if I won the first race on the Saturday I would secure the championship. Luckily, I did that and my father and uncle Graeme advised me to sit out the final race on Sunday to focus on my Supercars debut.

My co-driver in the second GRM car was sprintcar legend Max Dumesny and we managed to stay out of trouble throughout the race, although by the halfway mark the temperature inside the car was really starting to have an impact on me. With every lap it was getting hotter and hotter. I was desperately missing that natural airflow I was so used to in the Formula Ford.

While I was struggling near the end, we managed to get the Holden VX Commodore around safely enough to finish a couple of laps down in 20th. It got a tick from the boss as I was rewarded with a drive at Bathurst the following month.

Max wasn't so lucky as he was replaced by Mark Noske. I'd raced Formula Ford over the legendary Bathurst track previously, but trying to control a Supercar, which I still didn't really have a feel for, around Mount Panorama was going to be a challenge.

We qualified down the back of the field. Once again, the heat inside the car quickly became an issue and with each lap I started to get more and more concerned about my fitness.

I thought I was a fit 19-year-old and I'd actually been training since the start of 2002 when I joined Sonic Motorsport, as one of the first things they did was introduce me to a personal trainer.

His name was Anthony Klarica and Dad drove me to meet him, as he was working out of the Hawthorn Football Club at the time. He wrote me out a program that had me training six days a week.

It was eye-opening stuff – two 10km runs, two rides of

up to 50km, two swimming sessions, two gym workouts plus some stretching routines.

My father understood the ramifications of the moment, turning to me in the car on the way home and declaring, 'Mate, well, there goes your life,' as he laughed.

If I wanted to be a professional athlete and racecar driver, then fitness was going to play a huge part of it. This was something that was being rammed home to me as I battled to control this powerful beast of a Supercar around Bathurst.

There was clearly a difference between fitness and race fitness and I was struggling. I had this sense that I was *behind* the car. That sounds strange – it was just this sensation that I was hanging on.

The heat was extreme – it was 25 degrees hotter inside the car than the outside temperature, which meant I was in a confined space that was above 50 degrees. And I was dressed in a driving outfit that included a skivvy, underwear, a three-layered driving suit, boots, gloves and helmet.

We were almost three hours into the race on lap 73 when everything became too much. I was almost half-delusional when I clicked up into the wrong gear and locked the rear wheels up at the top of Mountain Straight, firing the car right into the fence.

I couldn't believe what I'd done. For that split second my body and mind had let me down, and the result was my first Bathurst race in a Supercar ending up in the fence.

By the time I got back to the pits I was convinced my career was over.

I knew my chances of getting a full-time driving gig next year were now extremely slim – and my options for anything else were limited. As a family we didn't have enough money to continue in Formula Ford, so maybe it was back to go-karting. Maybe I had to start thinking about life away from motorsport.

Thankfully, after the dust settled from the Bathurst disaster, Garry Rogers came through and offered me a drive for the 2003 season. Part of the deal was that I worked at his Melbourne car yard as a delivery driver and general handyman.

It was my first real job – I'd only done some shifts at my Dad's printing press previously – and I thought I was killing it given I was pursuing my dream and getting paid for it while picking up a few car parts on the side.

Being the rookie, I was understandably given the older car, with my teammate Garth Tander handed the new model Holden VY. It was hard work from the start, with the combination of my inexperience and an inferior car making life tough.

A big crash in New Zealand didn't help the confidence, but I got a golden opportunity to team up with Garth at Bathurst. In practice the car felt so good compared to what I was used to, but there was an issue that I anticipated was going to be a major problem on race day.

Garth was a lot taller than I was, which meant the driver's seat was in a difficult position. Actually, I could barely see over the steering wheel. Given that Garth was the No.1 driver, understandably it was locked in that position, and the team didn't have an appetite to change the seat position so it was just left where it was.

I was the rookie so I bit my tongue, but it was in the back of my mind and added to my stress levels, which were already high, given Garth had qualified us at the top end of the grid, in fourth position.

We had a quick car so a podium finish was the team's expectation. Garth got us off to a good start in his first stint. My job was to work my way back up through the field, given positions are obviously lost during a pit stop, and ensure we were back up near the lead when I handed over.

I'd quickly picked up a few spots and was attempting a pass around the kink just before Forest Elbow when disaster struck. The track drops away a bit at that point and because of the issue with my line-of-sight-from-the-seat situation I misjudged it, and before I knew it the car was spinning and going straight into the wall.

The front of the car was damaged and when I returned to the pits the crew had to push the radiator back into position. Unfortunately we went down several laps during the time it took to get the car fixed.

Any chance of a podium finish was gone and I was shattered as I sat on my own in the corner of the garage. Garry was staring at me from the other side with the biggest devil eyes. It is everyone's dream to win Bathurst – Garry had won before but wanted another one. He had put so much into it and I'd just ruined everything.

Looking back, I should've gone over and apologised right then and there and taken responsibility for what had happened. But I was still a kid, and sometimes when you're young you don't make the right decisions. I regret that now as I didn't conduct myself in the right way and definitely could have handled the situation differently.

I knew then and there that I wouldn't be driving for GRM the next year, and a month later Garry told me I was out of a job.

He called me into his office in the car yard and got straight to the point: 'We won't be using your driving services next year.'

I managed to hold it together but when I got into my car the tears started. I was in total disbelief: it felt like my life had been taken away from me. I'm not normally an emotional person but I couldn't control the tears. I was instantly overwhelmed with stress and anxiety about what the future was going to hold now.

The weird thing was there was still a couple of races left in the season, and I tried to look at that as a positive in that I could try and showcase my skills to prospective employers.

I went back to see Garry a week later because I had an employment contract until the middle of December. I needed to keep my job and I tried to talk him into letting me stay on in some fashion, but he wasn't keen other than to say I could wash cars in the dealership car yard for the rest of the year.

'Basically, you have to walk,' he said.

Where to? I was a 20-year-old who'd been given a golden opportunity and I'd blown it. And I soon found out what that meant: I was blacklisted.

Dad was onto me about ringing around the other teams to see if there were any opportunities. I found this so hard because I wasn't a salesman. I was no good at talking myself up and selling myself.

'Hi, it's Jamie. 'I'd love to drive your car if there are any opportunities available. I'm really good but have had the occasional crash.'

That just wasn't me, but Dad was relentless about it, so I kept plugging away on the phone. But it was obvious the word was out and no-one really wanted a bar of me.

So it was back to the family printing press to earn a few bucks before the help of my mate Paul Dumbrell saw Supercar legend Larry Perkins give me a chance with a test run at Winton.

His team ran three cars in the endurance events and I was supposed to do my trial in the third car, but something was wrong with it on the day so Larry told me to take the No.1 car, which was driven by Steve Richards, out for a few laps.

It was one of the best cars on the grid and I knew I had to take this opportunity, so I decided to let it rip. There was no use dawdling in such a powerful machine; I had to show them how I could drive fast and clean.

I managed to do the first bit but the second bit not so well, as on turn four I spun the car through the apex and backed it into the gravel trap.

As I sat in the gravel trap I couldn't believe what I'd done, what type of an idiot I was. Then I saw the track recovery vehicle come around, and in the passenger seat was Larry. I could tell by the way he flicked the door open that he was pissed! He was on a mission to get to the driver door as quickly as possible. I'm not sure if I was so bogged that the driver door wouldn't open, or that he chose not to open it, but he started – and didn't stop until he was finished – telling me I was the most useless human being in the country right then, through the little hole that's cut in the perspex window. I couldn't actually see his face – I was still strapped in with my helmet on and window net up – but I didn't need to to get the gist of his anger, with the words and spit spray coming into the cabin.

Another testing opportunity came up with a new team, Tasman Motorsport. It was at Oran Park Raceway in NSW and I was there battling it out with another rookie driver, Fabian Coulthard, for a spot in the endurance races.

I'd raced at Oran Park in 2003 and enjoyed the track. I felt very comfortable and actually ended up going quicker than I had on the race day the previous year. I hadn't wasted my time off, I'd actually kept studying the Supercar tracks and kept trying to understand the cars.

I wanted to know what the recipe for success was, and I was continually going over what I did right and, more importantly, what I did wrong and what was holding me back.

The test was well received by Tasman and they were keen to sign me up. Then suddenly I had a choice.

Remarkably after Larry had calmed down following the Winton incident, he was still keen for me to drive in the endurance events at Sandown and Bathurst.

This provided an interesting dilemma. Tasman were set to expand to two cars in 2005, so if I impressed them there was a big chance I'd secure a full-time drive the next season.

That scenario was unlikely with Perkins Motorsport, but I knew I would get a better result at Bathurst with them because they were one of the leading teams in the championship.

I figured if I performed well, then other doors could open on the back of that. It was a big risk – but I was playing the long game.

It wasn't how it had been sold to me, but I wasn't exactly in a position to complain after Larry Perkins decided to demote me to his third car for Bathurst.

I'd been expecting to team up with my mate Paul Dumbrell in the sister car that I'd put in the gravel trap, which had us dreaming of a possible podium finish.

But Larry had changed his mind and I'd been bumped down to the third car to drive with Alex Davison, who was also a good mate of mine, so that made the transition easier. And importantly, we worked together on the driver seat changes.

At the end of the 161 laps we felt like we'd won the race even though we'd actually finished tenth. To do that in the old third-string car was a sensational team performance and I felt like my punt was going to pay off.

There's a saying in motorsport that you're only as good as your last race, so I was thinking this kid was back.

With my confidence still sky high a couple of weeks later I rang Larry and asked if I could come and see him. When I got there he was out the back working on a car and while I was hoping to go into his office for a proper chat, he was showing no interest in that.

He barely stopped the machinery as I made my case.

'I thought I did a reasonable job and you mentioned there may have been something available. I was just wondering what that could be and if there's something available.'

'Nah mate, too many drivers, not enough cars.'

That wasn't the answer I was looking for. 'So, nothing available?' I asked again.

He shook his head and turned his attention back to the car he was fixing and that was the end of that.

Enter Tasman Motorsport. They were my last lifeline, so I quickly started working on trying to get that seat, which they'd threatened to withdraw after my Bathurst snub.

The team was New Zealand-based and run by Kevin Murphy, whose son Greg was a leading Supercar driver who'd won Bathurst in 2003. There were a number of shareholders, one of whom was Ron Harrop, the family friend who'd helped me out in Formula Ford.

However, there was a push to give a Kiwi the drive with several favouring Fabian Coulthard. I was pulling out all of the shots, so I suggested to Kevin that he ring Larry, who I assumed would give me a decent reference.

I was wrong.

Apparently, when quizzed about whether I was worth giving another shot to, Larry said: 'He's no good, he struggled under brakes and somehow they came tenth, I don't know how they did it.'

Luckily Kevin made another phone call to another Supercars legend, Jim Richards. He'd actually driven in the Bathurst race as a co-driver with his son Steve.

'What did you think of Jamie?' Kevin asked Richards.

His response was a much better one. He said that from what he could see and looking at the data, I'd done a really good job and considered me worthy of getting an opportunity.

I already liked Jim and that went to a whole new level when I found out about that conversation years later.

I was so grateful for the lifeline Tasman had given me and the best way to summarise the 2005 season was . . . bloody enjoyable.

An early highlight came when Supercars went on tour with a race held in Shanghai, China. It was a massive event with the eyes of the world watching, and I managed to finish fourth.

Jason Richards was Tasman's No.1 driver and we were partners for the endurance events. We both had a good sense of humour, and the combination gelled with my first podium finish at the Sandown 500, where we came in third, a huge feat for a small team like ours.

I thought that was going to be the highlight of the year but that was before we finished runner-up at Bathurst. It was an amazing day and I did the second-last stint – from lap 100 to 130 – and we were in third before overtaking the Triple Eight car, which had run into some mechanical issues.

The Holden Racing Team were out in front and I managed to close in on Todd Kelly. I was taking half-a-second each lap off him before they decided to pit. We had the car going beautifully, and at this stage it was suggested I should stay out and finish the race.

Then, at the last minute, there was a change of heart. I argued, because they'd just said I was staying out, but I think it was a bit of the Kiwi influence coming through and I was ordered into the pits to hand over to Jason.

When he came out, Tasman Motorsport were leading the Great Race. However, the reality was the Holden Racing Team's car, driven by Mark Skaife, had an extra 20 horsepower. Their straight-line speed was too much for us.

Our dreams of a surprise victory only lasted a few laps, with Skaife taking over the lead with 20 laps to go.

It had been an incredible event and one that would change my career forever.

A couple of days later I had a missed call from a Brisbane number. I rang it back and the voice at the other end said it was Roland Dane, the owner of Triple Eight Race Engineering.

'I want to see you,' Dane said.

'Where are you?' I asked.

'In Brisbane,' he replied.

'All right, I'll book a ticket and come and see you tomorrow.'

I thought it was a piss-take by one of my mates, so when I hung up I immediately googled the phone number. Sure enough, it was Triple Eight's headquarters.

They were an emerging outfit. Craig Lowndes had moved there at the start of 2005, and they'd shown near the end of the season they had a fast car and were a team in a hurry.

The meeting with RD, as everyone called him, went well and I really enjoyed the emphasis they put on the engineering side of the business. They didn't have to do a big sell. I was convinced straight away and told him pretty much that I was in and would do whatever it took to join Triple Eight.

They said they'd come back to me in a few days. But I got a call when I was still at Brisbane Airport saying the offer was in my email. It was a three-year deal on minimal money, but I didn't care about that, I would've done it for free.

There was an interesting twist a couple of days later when I returned to Melbourne. I received a call from Ford Performance Racing (FPR), who wanted to have a meeting.

Their headquarters was only 20 minutes from home and the team hierarchy of Rod Barrett and Tim Edwards put forward an impressive case. They knew about the Triple Eight offer and were prepared to try and blow it out of the water.

The money was considerably more, there was a company car involved and they were a factory-backed team who'd been way more successful than Triple Eight to this point.

And they were down the road from where I lived. Even though I was now 22 I'd never thought about leaving my parents, because life there was so easy. I'd never paid rent and never had to do anything, really, so it made much more sense on many levels to join FPR.

But I politely declined the offer. I was playing the long game.

3

YOU ARE THE AVERAGE OF THE PEOPLE AROUND YOU

SURROUNDING yourself with the right people is crucial in life, because you end up actually being the average of those people. So if you are striving to be better and the five people you hang around with are all happy with the easy life and aren't concerned with trying to be better, then you're never going to be better.

Everyone is different and some understandably will be happy with their lot in life and not be looking to improve it significantly. This is where you have to make a decision about what you want to do, where you want to go and how you want to live your life. It's smart to be wary of the company you keep because it will impact you.

I'm always trying to be better, to go bigger and expand, to learn new things and see different sides of things. I always want to keep moving forward and not get stuck in a rut, stuck in the same old day-to-day grind. I like spending time around people who are smarter and who have more knowledge in certain areas than me. These are the people who challenge you in a way that makes you better.

Friends are friends, family is family and you love spending time with them, but also make sure you get around people who challenge you and are the type of people who you strive to be. If you can find those people, I recommend spending time with them because it ends up brushing off on you.

This was a scenario I recognised the moment I walked into a Brisbane garage in 2006 and sat down next to two men who would shape my life over the next decade.

'So what are you up to next year?'

It was a loaded question to my best mate Will Davison as we cooled down after running the famous Tan Track in Melbourne. We'd been training together regularly over the summer and there were rumours circulating about both of us being on the move for the 2006 season.

Will had driven for the Dick Johnson Racing team in the endurance events and was hunting around for a more permanent seat.

'I'm looking at something, but I can't really say,' he said with a smile.

'Yeah, I'm the same.'

For a couple of awkward minutes we danced around the elephant in the room before I decided we were just being ridiculous.

'Between you and me, I've done a deal with Triple Eight and I'm moving to Brisbane,' I blurted out.

There was instant relief on his face. 'I've just done a deal with Dick Johnson Racing and I'm moving to the Gold Coast.'

We couldn't believe it. The scenario couldn't get any better. To be able to share this experience with a good mate who I'd grown up with, and who obviously understood the world of car racing, was perfect.

Call me soft but even though I was 23 the prospect of leaving home was daunting and it was particularly tough on Dad.

Will and I had flown up to Queensland and had a look around, settling on Hope Island, which was on the north side of the Gold Coast. It was a beautiful location and I didn't mind having to commute up to Triple Eight's headquarters in Brisbane.

I hired a trailer and filled the car with all of my belongings and hit the road. I had a passenger for the journey, with Dad declaring he was coming with me to set everything up.

No matter how much I missed home, I knew I had to keep my eyes forward and focus on all the good stuff that was going to happen with this change in my life.

Will and I both understood the fortunate positions we'd been placed in. While we still enjoyed ourselves, the enormity of the opportunity we'd been presented with to be professional drivers was not lost on us, we weren't out on the town every night; instead, we were focused on eating well and training to prepare ourselves for our dream job.

I'd trained so hard throughout January and February that I was convinced I was reporting to duty with Triple Eight in the best condition of my life.

This seemed to amuse my engineer Ludo Lacroix and the team's physio Chris Brady, who kept laughing as I continued to press the point.

I got the impression they'd heard it all before, but the main thing was that in my mind I was convinced I was ready, I'd done the work and deserved to be here.

I'd actually been advised not to be here at all. Playing second fiddle to Craig Lowndes had proven to be a poisoned chalice.

He was the star of the Supercars circuit, a three-time championship winner who'd moved to Triple Eight from the Ford Performance Racing team a year earlier and finished second in the 2005 championship.

Several industry figures had reached out and said: 'Just be careful. It's not a coincidence he's had seven different teammates in the last seven years.'

My Uncle Graeme also had some reservations, his theory being that he made all of his teammates look ordinary because he was so good and most of them either retired or had their careers ended.

Again, I'm not sure if it was my arrogance or this inner belief that I was ready, but none of this worried me. I thought if I was given good-enough equipment, then I could run with anyone. It was going to be a challenge and I was ready for it.

Lowndesy, who was nine years older than me, was nothing but helpful from the minute I walked into Triple Eight. What you see is what you get. That young kid personality and easygoing guy on the TV is exactly what he's like behind the scenes. He's a good genuine bloke who just loves motorsport and life in general.

He could have easily made it intimidating, made it hard for me to learn and transition into Supercars, but he went the other direction, going out of his way to make me welcome in the big time.

This was on show from my first gig as a Triple Eight driver when the team had an open day at the workshop and there were 500 fans there. They were all there to see Lowndesy. No-one knew who I was, but Lowndesy made sure he introduced them all to me and passed on every poster for me to sign as well, much to the disappointment of most of the fans I suspect.

The first race of the season was through the streets of Adelaide, the Clipsal 500, and expectations were low for me. Basically, I was the junior who they'd got cheap and I was to stay out of trouble and support Lowndesy for the endurance races.

I had other ideas.

The car was clearly the best Supercar I'd had the privilege to sit in and, in the opening race of the weekend, everything fell into place. I'd been up there in qualifying and transferred that to the race, finishing third with Lowndesy taking the win, which certainly pleased my new bosses.

That happiness continued in the following day's race when I found myself at the front of the pack after the opening 40 minutes. I couldn't believe I was leading the Clipsal 500. The car felt so balanced and I was just going with it.

Lowndesy ended up getting involved in an incident, so suddenly all the team's expectations were directed towards me in the No.88 car. Ludo was in my ear encouraging me the whole way, and I managed to hold it together to register my first Supercars race win.

And I also got to collect the Clipsal 500 trophy with my combined results being the best of the weekend.

I was overcome with relief initially, as I hadn't even dreamed of this, but as I told the media afterwards, this win was dedicated to giving young talent an opportunity. While winning one race doesn't mean much in the big picture, I felt like I was on top of the world.

The reality of this sport is that it soon comes back to bite you and we didn't return to the podium again until June, when I finished second at Winton. I then battled away with enough top 10 finishes to ensure the bosses didn't think the season-opening victory was a fluke.

Everything was geared towards the endurance events, which saw me cross over to the other side of the garage and work with Lowndesy's engineer and drive his car. This was what Roland Dane had employed me for, to work with the team's star, get through my stint in the car unscathed and keep us in a position to win.

I managed to do my part at Sandown, but our race strategy wasn't quite right and we had to settle for third behind the Ford Performance Racing team of Jason Bright and my go-kart adversary Mark Winterbottom.

Five days later, on 8 September 2006, the world of Australian motorsport was rocked with the death of Peter Brock.

He'd been the face of the sport, the much-loved charismatic figure who'd won Bathurst a record nine times. It hit everyone hard, but none harder than Lowndesy, who had been his protégé.

Brock had died during the Targa West road rally in Western Australia when the Daytona Coupe he was driving hit a tree. He was 61.

Lowndesy had known him all his life, as his father had worked as a mechanic and engineer for the man known as 'The King of the Mountain'. So when Lowndesy arrived on the scene as a fresh-faced kid with the Holden Racing Team, Brock was there to give him a guiding hand.

The pair were forever linked with Lowndesy quickly being hailed as the new Brock after winning the championship and the Bathurst 1000 at the age of 22 in 1996.

As a consequence, the build-up to Bathurst was bigger than usual with so much emotion associated with the race. It had a massive impact on Lowndesy, and the team weren't sure as we entered race week whether he was going to be able to drive.

In the qualifying session he seemed to be in control and got the 888 Ford Falcon into sixth position on the starting grid.

Race day was strange.

Before the start of the race, Lowndesy drove around the Mount Panorama track in the Holden Torana that Brock had driven in his first Bathurst victory, back in 1972. It was a moving tribute and then the whole of pit lane stood still for a minute's silence to honour the race's greatest ever combatant. It was the first and probably the last time I ever witnessed a proper minute's silence. Even though the hill was packed with race fans who had been drinking for a week straight, not one person said a word – even the birds stopped chirping. It was incredible.

And then when Peter's widow, Bev, hugged Lowndesy and told him the race was 'ours', he was in tears. It was tough to watch, seeing a friend in so much distress. RD had a chat with him and suggested it might be best if he took some time and let me start the race.

'Just take an hour to get your head right,' RD said.

He wouldn't have a bar of it and almost in an instant he flicked the switch and went from emotional Craig to determined Craig.

I'm not a spiritual person, I have no religious beliefs apart from eating Easter eggs. I don't believe there is some weird force going on or someone has written a script that we're all following, but gee, it was a crazy day.

Everything that needed to go right did go right and anything that could go wrong didn't go wrong. It was eerie, the car didn't miss a beat and I was swept up by this weird force and produced one of the best driving stints of my career.

We'd managed to avoid some early carnage and on the second-last stint I managed to claim the lead from Todd Kelly off a safety car restart on lap 110.

When I handed over to Lowndesy for the final time, we had the lead and there was never any doubt what was going to happen next. He was inspired, and to add to the spookiness, the winning margin over Rick and Todd Kelly was just 0.5 of a second – the same number, 05, which Peter Brock had made famous throughout his career.

Understandably, by the time Lowndesy got back to the presentation area, he was again in tears.

I was proud to win my first Bathurst crown but this day was all about my mate. I was just forever grateful that I'd been able to play a part in this special day for him and to hold the inaugural Peter Brock Trophy – which had been presented by Brock's brother Phil – alongside him.

You won't be surprised to learn that was easily the highlight of my debut year at Triple Eight. We ended up finishing tenth in the championship, which was quite funny given how that number had been at the front of my mind a few months earlier.

The contract I'd quickly signed to get my big break had in the fine print a clause that said there was an automatic renewal for the next year if I finished top 10 – but if I was 11th it was not guaranteed.

Thankfully, the Bathurst result took care of that with RD coming up to me afterwards to give me the heads up that I was guaranteed a seat in 2007. That avoided a lot of angst as in the final round at the Phillip Island Circuit I blew up an engine in the last of the three races. Even with that dose of bad luck, I still ended up having a dozen or so points up my sleeve from 11th-placed James Courtney.

But as a team we had bigger things to worry about at Phillip Island.

Lowndesy was level on points with Rick Kelly coming into the final race of the year at the Victorian circuit, which is also home to the Australian Motorcycle Grand Prix.

There had been some aggro between the two teams in the first two races with Kelly's HSV Dealer Team doing their best to block Lowndesy at every opportunity.

Then in the decider Kelly clipped Lowndesy heading into the hairpin, spearing him off the track. The crash forced the 888 car into the pits for a lengthy stop, where the crew desperately tried to repair the damage. Kelly received a drive-through penalty for the incident, but he was still able to finish the race in 18th position to seal the championship victory, while Lowndesy limped into 29th, four laps down.

We were fuming and RD immediately lodged a protest. It was over the next few hours I realised I'd made the right decision. Everyone else had packed up and left, but the entire Triple Eight team sat there and waited for the stewards hearing.

It would've been easy to go down to the pub and grab a counter meal after the final race of the season, but the championship meant so much to every member of the team that we all stood around and waited for hours.

Eventually, the stewards came out with the decision that they needed more time. (The following day our protest was dismissed.) In that moment I got to see what teamwork really meant and what Triple Eight were all about.

I was surrounded by the right people.

'Don't let great get in the way of good.'

That was one of the many inspirational quotes my engineer Ludo Lacroix would throw my way, but it was the one that resonated the most.

The relationship between driver and engineer is the most important one in the entire team. Being able to communicate every last detail about the car is so important in striving to make it faster.

Ludo took me under his wing the minute I walked in and changed my view of motorsport. I'd been more focused on the driving component and didn't have a real understanding of the engineering side of the business and what goes into mechanically getting a racecar ready.

He would continually challenge me to learn, to be a better person and driver through more knowledge. I thrived in that environment.

Ludo's work ethic was incredible; he would do whatever it took to make the racecar faster. While he was always searching for perfection, he had this amazing ability to understand what was practical in every situation.

His theory about not letting great get in the way stuck. If you relate it to a small part for the car: if you've got one that's good then put it on the car that weekend, test it, refine it and make it better. Don't hold off until that particular part, or particular idea, is great because it could take weeks or even months to get it to the point of perfection.

If you're always waiting until something is absolutely great to put in a racecar then you will be behind the eight ball, you won't be able to move forward as fast as you'd like. Getting something good and making it great over time was a lesson in life that stuck from my crazy French engineer.

At the start of 2007 Ludo decided he wanted to expand his horizons and change his focus to the performance and direction of the team as a whole. That meant stepping away from being my engineer to instead put his energy into creating and building a new car for Triple Eight, which was an exciting move.

His replacement was Mark Dutton, who'd been our data engineer, so I'd already spent a lot of time with him. We clicked immediately. In many respects he was in a similar situation to me: he was a young guy who was desperate to get an opportunity to show his skills.

Dutto really simplified things and listened more to what I had to say. That's not a criticism of Ludo – he was obviously so experienced in doing the job that he would generally end up doing it his way despite my feedback.

But with Dutto we quickly fell into a rhythm of understanding. For example, if we were trying out a spring and I said the softer one felt better then that was the way we would go, even if the theory suggested a stiffer spring was the best bet. Ludo would often side with the theory; Dutto was more likely to side with the feel of the driver.

Dutto brought a lot of common sense, he didn't get too technical and instead focused on getting the basics right and doing them really well. It was a recipe for success, because straight away in 2007 we had a car that was a serious contender.

And for the first time the car was set up for my style.

Drivers go fast in different ways. There are literally a hundred different combinations in the engineering process to accommodate a driver's style.

Generally there are drivers who prefer a 'good front', which is when the front of the car controls everything and an extension of that is some actually like the front to slide. Then there are other drivers who prefer the back part of the car to be more dominant and have more grip.

When I arrived at Triple Eight I just copied Lowndesy. He was the star of the show, so it made sense that I was just going to follow his lead. I would pour over his data from every session and compare it to my data, because I thought I needed to perfect his style of driving. But it wasn't natural to me. And if I then tried to drive it my own way, the car wasn't set up right so that simply didn't work.

I'm more what you'd call a neutral. Lowndesy is one extreme where he wants the front of the car to be what we call 'on the nose'. If you look at him coming into a corner, he is able to turn inside and hook into a corner with extreme speed, but that means he's not as fast coming out.

At the other end of the spectrum is someone like Garth Tander, who comes into the corner very wide for the turn but then gets on the gas and the car is like a rocket coming out of it, which enables him to fly down the straight.

I'm in the middle, not extreme one way or the other. I'd spent my first year in a car that was all about the front like Lowndesy, but with the help of Dutto we started to shape the car more for my style.

And the results came quickly. We were on and around the podium in the first half of the season but Tander was well in front until we hit the endurance races, where Lowndesy and I again dominated, winning Sandown and going back-to-back at Bathurst.

The rain hit late in the race at Bathurst, and I nervously watched the final hour as cars slid all over the place with Lowndesy locked in an epic battle with Steven Johnson of Dick Johnson Racing. Once again, he showed his class and experience to pull off a stunning pass and then go on to hold the advantage to the chequered flag.

It was obviously a less emotional victory than 12 months earlier, but it suddenly put a potential championship in the frame.

There were a few ups and downs to follow, but when I took two wins and Tander crashed out in the final race of the penultimate event in Tasmania, I found myself with a chance to steal the championship.

That's how it felt, the HSV Dealer Team had been clearly quicker overall throughout the year but there was an opening, so everything came down to the three races at Phillip Island for Triple Eight.

It was cut-throat racing in the first two races, with the HSV Dealer Team desperate to ensure Tander got his hands on the trophy. He won the opening races at Phillip Island while I could only manage third in both. It meant he had the lead going into the final race, but there was only a handful of points between us.

Fittingly, it came down to the last couple of laps. Tander was in fourth position after Lowndesy had done the team thing and lunged at him to execute a brilliant pass to get into third. I was in second place, with the scenario being I had to pass Todd Kelly to win the championship.

Unfortunately I didn't have the pace on the day and had to settle for second, which meant I finished the season on 623 points – just two points shy of Tander. Lowndesy finished third on 592 points.

After the initial disappointment subsided, the fact I was runner up in the championship in just my second year at Triple Eight and third full season as a driver was incredible.

Importantly, the man who mattered the most in my career at that stage agreed.

Roland Dane approached me not long after the end of the season and tore up my contract. I'd originally signed on for three years, basically on apprentice's money, and that included the coming year, 2008.

But given what I just achieved RD said that wasn't fair. He wanted to pay me what he thought I was worth, rather than what it said on the contract.

And that's why I have so much respect for the man. Good people do good things.

It was only a flicker in the mirror. And in that split second I knew I was in trouble.

Qualifying is all about speed. All my focus was on nailing down pole position for the opening race of the Hamilton 400 in New Zealand when I zoomed up on the inside of Todd Kelly, who'd run off the track at turn five.

It was a regulation move and I was focused on continuing what was already my fastest run of the day when I saw it.

Kelly had regained control and was pulling back onto the track, seemingly oblivious to the fact I was now on his inside. It was the slightest bump to my rear wheel, but when you're travelling over 200kph, that's all it takes.

Before I knew it, my Ford Falcon was spearing straight into the wall. There was no time to brake or even brace for the impact and it was a big hit.

Crashes are an occupational hazard in my business, but I'd been relatively lucky throughout the early stages of my career.

The biggest one I'd had to deal with happened in a Formula Ford, although it probably lives in the memory bank more for what it could've potentially meant, rather than the actual crash itself.

It was back in 2000 and I went wide on a turn at Phillip Island and cannoned into the safety barrier of tyres, completely trashing the side of the car. We'd used all of the family money to buy that new Ford and I'd gone and almost written it off.

All my thoughts on that day had been about how I could have just blown up my career right there and then, because I didn't know if we could afford to fix the car.

This time, my thoughts were about what it all meant for the rest of the weekend – I'd got through the crash unscathed, but the car was a mess.

It had slammed into the wall front-on initially, but then because of the massive amount of g-force I'd careered backwards into the other wall.

There was significant damage everywhere, and by the time

I got back to the pits, I had an uneasy feeling about whether the car was salvageable.

My worst fears were soon confirmed.

The chassis had been bent. While the Triple Eight mechanics were geniuses, there was no way they would be able to get that car back on track, which was a disaster.

In a championship race, to wipe out an entire weekend – three races, which amounts to 300 points – usually meant the year was gone.

The Hamilton debacle certainly put a dampener on what had been a great start to 2008, given I'd won the Clipsal 500 in Adelaide for a second time to open the season and was in the championship lead coming into the third event in NZ.

There was added expectation now, and the feeling was nothing but a championship was the appropriate result for Triple Eight, who had never tasted the ultimate success yet.

The mentality had changed within the team. I was no longer the rookie backup, I was a championship contender who was now on par with Lowndesy.

That said a lot about Lowndesy and RD, because that certainly wouldn't be the case in every garage. The established star would always get the preferential treatment, but there was an equality from the start of 2008.

Triple Eight now had two No.1 drivers.

We shared data, the cars were identical and the only thing that made the difference on race day was which driver and engineer were getting the most out of their car. Confirmation of the partnership came at Bathurst when, for the first time, Lowndesy came over to my side of the garage.

Previously we'd used his engineer and mechanics for the Great Race, but this time around Dutto was going to be in charge, along with my mechanics Garry Bailey and Ty Freele.

A slice of history was on offer for us, with only two other teams winning Bathurst in three consecutive years – Peter Brock–John Richards (1978, '79, '80) and Peter Brock–Larry Perkins (1982, '83, '84). I didn't really allow myself to think about potentially joining the sport's all-time greats, but there was a feeling everything was coming together at the right time for Triple Eight.

It was almost the perfect storm.

The cars that we'd built were seriously fast, we had the best engineers, Lowndesy and I were pushing each other to be better, and commercially the team was thriving with the support of major sponsor Vodafone. Everything was coming together.

We qualified fifth on the starting grid and by lap 34 Lowndesy had the lead. We were never really threatened after that, with my veteran teammate showing his experience over the final 10 laps to hold off challenges from Greg Murphy and James Courtney.

I was stunned for words when a television camera was thrust in front of me just after Lowndesy had crossed the line to put our names in the history books.

'It's unbelievable, '06 was something else, '07 was even better and this is amazing. I'm not a greedy person but I'll take it,' I said. 'This place is amazing, this is where all my dreams have come true. How good was Lowndesy in the last stint? He just does it and nails it every time.'

And what my third Bathurst win also did was put me back at the top of the championship race with four rounds remaining, which was crazy given I thought we were gone six months earlier.

The lead was now 32 points over Mark Winterbottom and that perfect storm I'd sensed leading into Bathurst turned into a Triple Eight tsunami over the next few weeks.

That elusive first championship victory for RD became a reality after I managed to win nine of the next 10 races in Surfers Paradise in Queensland, Bahrain in the Persian Gulf, Symmons Plains in Tasmania and then officially claiming it in the opening race of the final weekend at Sydney's Oran Park.

Relief was the first emotion.

That was quickly followed by excitement for RD and the team, who'd worked so hard to finally get Triple Eight at the top of Australian motorsport. The celebrations were big but I already had my eye on my own little getaway.

For my entire life my family had gone to Corowa on the Murray River for summer holidays, and I couldn't think of a better place to reflect on what had been a whirlwind three years as a full-time professional racecar driver.

I'd never really stopped and thought about what I'd achieved given my mentality had always been, even back in go-karts, to focus on the next race.

There were so many people who'd helped me along the way and at the top of the list was my father. But there was also the rest of my family, friends, engineers, mechanics and team owners who'd all played a part.

It also made me realise that in life there's always someone better off and always someone worse off. I'd just won a Supercars Championship at the age of 25, I was at the top of the world in regards to my career.

Did it mean I should look to Formula 1? My good mate Will Davison had a crack a few years earlier but it didn't work out. It seemed to be the obvious progression for someone who'd made it to the top of their domestic competition. But why do we always think immediately about people who are better off or about making more money?

Sure, it might help you to want to strive to be better, but then at the same time there are plenty of friends and young kids I raced go-karts against who had just as much talent as me but never got the same opportunities.

Obviously you have to make the most of your opportunities and work hard to generate them. But there are other people who've worked just as hard as I have, who haven't been in the right place at the right time and got the opportunity to come through with the best team in the country and win a Supercars Championship.

We all aspire towards happiness but what is complete happiness? No-one really knows, and while we continue to hunt for that, the key is to be respectful of the good things you have now and appreciate them.

I certainly did that during my three-week break in the caravan by the river, with a bit of water skiing thrown in. It was exactly the tonic needed to attempt to recharge the batteries, although I quickly figured out that tasting championship success just fuelled me to go again.

Pre-season training began early in 2009 and it was obvious our team was on the hunt for perfection. It was exciting to have the fastest car on the grid, but we weren't content with that.

There were always tweaks to improve the car's performance and really that sums up the life of a racecar driver – taking something good and trying to make it better. To stay at the top, we had to be innovative and start thinking outside the square.

We understood there were other teams copying our technology, so we had to work out how to be better, how to be fitter and how to drive faster.

And our point of difference in 2009 was a brand-new FG Ford Falcon, which for the first time Triple Eight had built. Previously the bodywork was provided and we then had to add all the finishing touches. Being able to design our own bodywork – which was what my former engineer Ludo had been doing for a couple of years – meant we could determine the aerodynamic package for the car. There was an overall downforce and drag number under the regulations, but it was up to each team whether they did it at the front or rear of the vehicle.

It was all part of the determination to prove to the rest of the grid that we weren't resting on our laurels. We showed that in devastating fashion with Triple Eight winning the first six races of the 2009 season.

I repeated my success in Adelaide at the Clipsal 500 and then won both races in Hamilton, New Zealand, with Lowndesy taking the chocolates at Winton in the third event of the year.

The build-up to Bathurst was even bigger than usual with Lowndesy and I shooting for a history-breaking four wins in a row.

It turned out to be the last time we were going to team up. A change of rules introduced at the end of the year barred each team's two main drivers pairing up in the endurance races. The reasoning was sound as it meant the elite talent was spread throughout the grid, which theoretically would see more legitimate contenders at Mount Panorama.

Unfortunately we didn't get the opportunity to go out with a bang. A clutch problem over the final 40 laps meant we never got a chance to challenge properly, and ended up finishing fifth behind my good friend Davo, who was now part of the Holden Racing Team setup with Garth Tander.

I'd learnt so much from Lowndesy and when people asked what he was like I told them, what you see on the TV is what you get. He always had a smile on his face, and on the rare occasion that he was feeling down, there was a distinct signal.

When Lowndesy started singing 'Oh My Darling Clementine' to himself, you gave him a wide berth because it meant someone had really pissed him off.

My funniest Lowndesy story – and there have been many – involved Australian supermodel Jennifer Hawkins. She visited the Triple Eight garage before the start of the 2008 Clipsal 500 and everyone was in awe of the former Miss Universe.

But not Lowndesy.

'Hey Jen, how ya going?' he said as he gave her a big hug.

He then told her she should have a seat in a Supercar, so he helped her slide in, which was all good, but it was when she wanted to get out that trouble struck.

'How do I get out?' Jennifer asked.

Lowndesy told her to sit tight and proceeded to try and detach the steering wheel, which was designed to slip in and out.

But the harder he pulled the more resistant it seemed to be. Then suddenly it gave way and the wheel smacked Jennifer in the face.

We tried not to lose it and Lowndesy was horrified. To Jennifer's credit she brushed it off and said she was fine, but there was no doubt it would've stung.

That was classic Lowndesy. No-one else could've gotten away with it.

My sense of humour was tested in the next event on the Gold Coast, where a brain fade saw me crash out in the third race of the weekend.

It was a reality check of sorts because I'd started to feel a bit tired and my motivation had slipped down a notch. I was probably more on autopilot, expecting things to happen because we had a fast car rather than really fighting for it. I hadn't had a decent break after 2008 because I'd been so pumped about the new season, and it was starting to take its toll.

This was a crash that wouldn't have happened if I was on my game. There were only four laps to go. I was in a good position in the top five, looking at some decent points, when

I lost concentration as I came across a lap car and slammed into the wall.

The front of my FG Ford was badly smashed up and there was also damage to the rear, which was a disaster given the final race through the streets of Surfers Paradise was only 90 minutes away.

There is nothing worse than the feeling of knowing you'd just ruined all the great work of the team – not to mention it cost the boss more than $150,000 in repairs. You never want to be the weakest link, but that day I felt like I was.

This was where I once again got an insight into the strength of the Triple Eight outfit, because at no stage did they consider the car wasn't going to be on the start line for race four.

It was a typically hot Gold Coast day and the temperature in the garage was boiling. The car was still scorching hot from having done a 100km race, yet there were mechanics almost burning their hands because they knew the clock was ticking.

There were at least 20 people working on the car with people from other teams coming in to lend a hand. Dutto and I would normally be talking about strategy in the lead-up to a race but we were both getting our hands dirty, pulling things off the car and hammering things into place.

It was totally crazy and because of the crash I started the final race in last place on the grid. I was still very sheepish about what I'd done and was wondering what my plan of attack was when RD approached to wish me good luck, which he did before every race.

'What do you want me to do here, boss?' I asked. 'What's the strategy? Do you want me to just bring it home nice and clean because of what's already happened?'

He just stared straight back at me and said: 'Don't come back unless you're in the top five.'

It was one of the greatest things I'd ever heard and said so much about the man and the team. He didn't care about what had happened, he didn't care about the cost, all he cared about was the racing.

These fighting words completely changed my mentality instantly. From the moment the lights dropped I went hard like a madman, which isn't easy to do on the Gold Coast track because it is so tight, yet I passed eight cars in the opening two laps.

A red flag complicated things as it meant I had to drop back to my starting position again but there was no stopping me. I was inspired and produced one of the best drives of my life to finish fifth.

That effort from the entire team, and RD in particular, would end up being the reason I went on to win my second drivers' championship.

I was surrounded by the right people.

4

KEEP IT REAL

WHY do we care so much about what other people think?

I love animals – except maybe black-headed pythons but more about that later – partly because they don't care about what others think. You watch dogs running around the park – they don't care if they're barking too loud or rolling around in their own business.

Whereas we humans, we're worried about whether you can wear tracksuit pants outside. And if you're a woman in particular, the pressure to look good is constantly there. When I was at school I convinced my parents into buying me a pair of Doc Martens shoes. I simply had to wear Doc Martens to school because that's what everyone else did – and if I didn't, then I wouldn't be cool. It felt like a matter of life or death if I didn't get these $150 pair of shoes.

And for Free Dress Day I got Mum to take me to Rebel Sport to buy a Michael Jordan singlet so I could wear it over my T-shirt, because that was what the cool kids were doing. Looking back, I regret following trends and trying to be somebody I wasn't.

These days I make sure I don't make the same mistake and fall into the same trap. I dress the way I want to dress and I almost go to the extreme other end of the spectrum. If there's something that's remotely on trend – even if I actually like the trend – I make sure I stay away from it to prove to myself that I'm not succumbing to peer pressure. I just try to be myself and I guess that's where I've adopted my motto in life, which is to 'keep it real'. That's what I live by and what I try to do.

There's so much fakeness in this world, and you can get caught up in believing that if you do X, then people will have more respect for you. I hate all of that stuff. I just want to be honest and straight up about who I am. The reality is not everyone's going to like it; in fact, there are more that probably don't like it, but at the end of the day I have to go home and look in the mirror and have self-respect. I have been real, I haven't been someone else, I haven't been fake and I've played a straight bat, which is of huge value to me.

As I've grown older, wiser and more experienced, I've continued this push towards the truth. If you're true to yourself, then my philosophy is that the people who matter don't mind and the people who do mind don't matter.

This isn't overly easy in the sporting world and it was a stance that had me on the outer, at a time when my career was starting to take off.

*

'How dare you not stop. We'd waited two hours.'

Welcome to another day on social media. This one was a Facebook message from an angry mother because apparently I'd ignored her little Johnny and didn't sign his poster when I was on my way to start a race.

Obviously I didn't see little Johnny, or it was at an inappropriate time where my focus was on getting to the garage to prepare for what I was paid to do.

Unfortunately this had become a regular thing. I was getting attacked more and more on social media and while I told people I didn't look at it, I did have a scroll every now and then. I certainly had an understanding of what was going on. While there was a little bit of frustration, I was more trying to understand what was causing it.

To be fair, I didn't help myself.

The thing was, I didn't sign up to be a good guy. I didn't sign up to be a role model and I certainly didn't sign up to be a media performer.

In my mind I signed up to drive a Supercar as fast as I possibly could and to work with a team to design and build a car that wins Triple Eight races.

As more attention came my way with the more races I started to win, I didn't handle the media very well. If anything, I went out of my way to do a bad job. My theory – which in hindsight was ridiculous – was that if I did a bad job then they wouldn't want to talk to me again.

In reality, I was making it very easy for the fans and the public to hate me. I did a really good job of giving someone who might have a 50–50 view on me every opportunity to say: 'He's a wanker.'

People said I was arrogant. I was. I don't regret that and I certainly don't regret doing whatever I needed to do to get the most out of myself because that helped me to win championships. But there was no gain for me to do a bad job in the media and come across in a way that wasn't really me. There are interviews I'd watch back years later and cringe at how I'd behaved.

The problem was I didn't have the skills back then to deal with it. Ironically I had the perfect person beside me to learn from.

Craig Lowndes was the ultimate fan favourite, loved far and wide by everybody. He'd learnt how to deal with the spotlight by leaning on the greatest of all time, Peter Brock. So he put a big emphasis on his media profile and fan interaction, whereas that was a low emphasis in my books.

I simply had it in my head that if I drove the racecar as fast as I possibly could and provided entertainment for people then I was doing my job. I hoped they would be inspired by somebody taking this 600-horsepower piece of machinery to the racetrack and trying to get the most out of it.

I thought the drama of making mistakes, coming up short and then trying again excited the fans. Things like ending up in the gravel trap, hitting the wall, crashing into somebody, getting a drive-through penalty and even losing a tyre.

I hoped people were entertained by someone trying to explore the limits, which is what we did every race weekend. We were out there exposing ourselves and being vulnerable because we were having a crack, and if someone was having a couple of beers on the couch on a Sunday afternoon watching a dog-eat-dog Supercars duel to the very end, then that was real entertainment.

That was my job.

I figured the biggest reward for the fans and the best thing I could do for the sport was to provide that entertainment. To drive fast and win races – and I'm not sure I was capable of doing that and always getting out of the car and being Mr Nice Guy.

It can be very tough because at times you've got a fan base that actually wants something different to what you're genuinely feeling in that particular moment. A lot of them would like to see me get out of the car and say: 'Oh it wasn't quite our day, we tried our best but there's always next year.'

If I said that I'd go home that night, look in the mirror and say: 'You spun some shit to be Mr Popular.'

I wouldn't be true to myself, I'd be cheating myself to try and look good in front of others and say what I thought people wanted to hear, rather than actually telling the truth.

This was why I started being called 'Jamie Whingecup' on social media.

If an official made a decision that stuffed up a race, for example a flag marshal was too slow doing their job, then I would say it. If that's how I feel, that's what I say. Bad luck if I step on some toes.

That wasn't whinging, that was just calling it as I saw it, because at the end of the day I love the sport and I want what's best for it. If there are issues I'll highlight them and, more importantly, I won't be fake.

There are other drivers on the grid who play up to the camera and try to come across as the good guy. It's cringe-worthy and so fake. I refuse to do that because I just have to keep it real.

However, my lack of filter would often get me in trouble and I made some comments midway through 2009 that did come back to bite.

'I won't retire at thirty. Whether I'll still be driving a racing car after thirty is another thing,' was the line I'd used during an interview.

When pressed further I said: 'Because there's a lot more to life than motorsport. It's something I live and breathe; I'll always be involved in motorsport in some way . . . but there's a lot out there. Hopefully I can look at this motorsport thing, tick that box and say, "hey, that's the majority of my life".

'But there are other challenges out there that I'd love . . . When I get to 60 and I'm old and my kids are wheeling me out in my wheelchair at the retirement village, hopefully I can say I've done a lot more than just won a V8 Supercars Championship.'

Naturally, these comments became a bigger deal than I'd imagined. Looking back, they probably reflect the fatigue I was starting to feel.

And I was about to get thrown another curveball.

This whole world of negativity and social media backlash really ramped up when it was revealed Triple Eight was leaving Ford and joining Holden.

To understand the gravity of such a move you have to go back decades. Growing up, you were either blue for Ford or red for Holden. It was one of the biggest rivalries in Australian sport and divided friends and sometimes even families. Once you picked a side, you were on it for life.

This domestic war had preceded Supercars and made household names of drivers because of which cars they raced. Dick Johnson was always Ford, while Peter Brock was obviously a Holden man.

So when there was a defection, it stirred up a lot of passion.

The reality was Ford had decided they didn't want to sponsor Triple Eight any longer as they were scaling back their Supercars commitments. They only wanted to support one team and that was obviously their factory team, Ford Performance Racing.

Holden were very keen to have us, and coincidentally RD had come to Australia back in 2004 from Britain with the intention of buying the Holden Racing Team. He'd had an association with Holden's sister company, Vauxhall, with his racing team in the UK. But HRT wasn't up for sale and instead he bought Briggs Motor Sport, which was a Ford team, so that meant he had to become a Ford man.

Triple Eight's move certainly raised tensions and we bore the brunt of an angry Ford fan base. A day didn't go by where we weren't called 'dogs' or 'traitors'.

The funny thing was the Holden fans were so used to hating us that they didn't exactly embrace us at the start either. It meant Lowndesy and I were in a weird place at the beginning of this new Supercars chapter.

RD's way of looking at it was that we would be going through a bit of short-term pain for long-term gain.

Changing manufacturers was a massive logistical exercise with so many challenges, and that's why what happened in Abu Dhabi ranks as one of the proudest moments of my career.

For the first time Supercars had its season-opener outside of Australia, with a double header in the Middle East. The first event of 2010 was at the Yas Marina Circuit in the United Arab Emirates, with the second round in Bahrain a week later. It was a massive deal for the sport, which previously had raced overseas only in China and New Zealand.

It was a magnificent operation in Abu Dhabi, with a large spacious track, all under lights. There was a lot of international eyes on the event, which is why RD was so pumped that we'd shown off our new Holdens to the world in style by winning both races.

We went to Bahrain and took the points there too, but it turned out these victories gave us a false sense of security, as we soon discovered in Adelaide at the Clipsal 500.

The Holden product was obviously new to us and we were still learning about it – and sometimes you learn the hard way. Adelaide is a tight track with lots of brushes on walls and the like. When I got a slight tap from behind during the race, the back of the car suddenly started falling off.

We ended up being black-flagged and copped a drive-through penalty for the flapping bumper bar. The Holden bodywork was a lot different to what we'd been used to with Ford and it kept catching us out at inappropriate times throughout the season.

But Holden certainly got their day in the sun at Bathurst with a classic 1-2 finish by Triple Eight.

In the first year of the big split, with each team's main drivers being separated for the endurance events, it was Lowndesy who won the race. My co-driver was Steve Owen and Lowndesy was partnered with Mark Skaife.

We made a good effort to stay close, and while I tried to reel Lowndesy in over the final couple of laps it was obvious it wasn't going to happen. So I got on the radio as we were going up Mountain Straight for the final time and suggested a parade finish.

It was an iconic image with the two Triple Eight cars crossing the line virtually together to celebrate Lowndesy's fifth victory at Mount Panorama.

The championship turned out to be a head-to-head war with Ford's James Courtney from the Dick Johnson Racing team, who interestingly enough were basically running with the Triple Eight cars from the previous year.

In a sense I felt like I was racing myself from last year as we'd built both DJR cars along with our own at the start of the 2009 championship. They did a great job refining their package, but essentially it was the same car.

Throughout 2010 I was convinced we had the quicker car, but we kept making errors, like putting too much fuel in for one race and then having the front bumper basically fall off in another.

The championship came down to the final weekend in Sydney on the Homebush Street Circuit. In the first race

I was locked in an epic struggle with Courtney and Mark Winterbottom.

Bad weather was the problem and we needed to make a call about when I would come in to change tyres. We had to weigh up whether it was quicker to run on slicks (the current tyres) for another lap when it started to rain and then come in for the wets (specially designed tyres for wet conditions), or put the wets on straight away and get them warm before the rain came.

Dutto decided I should stay out for one more lap – it might not be the fastest but it will give us a bit of security. The issue was the rain was torrential by the time we were at the back section of the circuit.

The cars were out of control and in perfect sequence as we all aquaplaned into the wall. Courtney, Winterbottom and I crashed one after the other. This was the classic Matt White and Mark Skaife commentary: 'They're all in the fence!' From that point it became a race to see who could get back to the pits first.

I managed to keep my car going whereas Courtney, who had the championship lead, initially struggled to get his Ford started again. We had a couple of minutes up our sleeve by the time he did get going, and from there it became a race to see who could get their car back out on the track to finish the race.

With the title race so tight, any points were valuable and getting even 10 points for finishing last was suddenly the priority. The key was you had to complete a final lap. In hindsight, our team did too good of a job fixing up my mangled Holden. Rather than just quickly slam it together like the other teams had done, my car was ready to do another 200km race.

Unfortunately we didn't get it out of the garage in time while Courtney managed to crawl his way to the line finishing 15th and getting a handful of points, which could have been the difference in the championship.

The following day I finished well ahead of him – fifth to 14th – but the damage was done and the title was his with 3055 points compared to my 2990.

We were devastated at not achieving three-in-a-row. In 2007 when I came second I always had the feeling that it wasn't mine to win but 2010 was completely different, that was my championship. But we dropped the ball and only had ourselves to blame.

As a result I was in a hole at the end of 2010.

The extreme intensity of our push to be the best had taken its toll. From the long grind of winning my first championship to the disruption of changing from Ford to Holden and then learning how a new car operated. And now throw in the body blow of missing out on a Supercars Championship that we clearly should've won.

It was time to check out. The regular Corowa stay was extended to four weeks and it was a motorsport blackout for me, not even my go-to website Auto Action was getting read.

Chilling out and some good rest was required as I came to terms with the reality that I wasn't the young kid on the block anymore. That had worn off and, as is the case in Australia, the tall poppy syndrome was taking effect.

Australians generally don't like people at the top, especially those who have a mentality like mine and a seemingly easy-to-dislike personality. It felt like any slip-up or controversial comment I made spurred the fans on to go harder and try to knock me from my perch.

I didn't need much spurring on for the 2011 season – it was all about redemption. If I needed any sort of jolt it came when I was back in the workshop and saw the No.88 getting put back on the car.

The Supercars custom had the reigning champion going with No.1 on his car the following year. So seeing that being replaced by the new lower-ranked number certainly added more fuel to the fire.

It sparked a response, as the No.88 car was on the podium in nine of the opening 11 races, which included five wins, while Lowndesy then produced a mid-season spurt that had both Triple Eight cars sitting first and second on the championship table.

My co-driver at Bathurst was a great mate of mine, Andrew Thompson, a former champion Formula Ford driver, who I'd hung out a lot with since I moved to Queensland.

There was still a lot of discussion around the new rules for the endurance races, which had come in the previous year. It made sense, given some of the stories you used to hear about how teams would put everything into its main car with the second car basically told to stay out of the way.

Each car is allocated eight sets of tyres at Bathurst and there were stories that some cars were getting through on three sets of tyres and therefore the main car with the No.1 driver would have an extra five brand-new sets of tyres to use for testing and practice before the next race meetings.

So having everyone put all their eggs in the one basket meant you only ended up having, say, 12 of the 25 cars on the grid with realistic chances of winning, whereas the normal scenario has most eligible.

Being able to give Thommo a leg-up in his career was one of my focuses at Bathurst. I knew he was placing everything he had into his own driving career, so I was desperate to help put his name up in lights at the biggest race on the calendar.

We were on track as it soon became obvious we had a seriously fast car that saw us right at the pointy end for most of the race. With 40 laps to go we were in the lead when suddenly a light flicked on in the dashboard.

That is never a good thing. Its message was confusing. It was suggesting that the battery was going flat but the car seemed to be operating at full capacity. What I didn't know was that the alternator issue, which then effected the battery, had turned the radio off, so I couldn't hear the team yelling at me to pit.

I'd sailed past them on Pit Straight, completely oblivious to the frantic scenes that were unfolding in the garage. They knew what was happening but had no way of communicating it to me. I was going to pit the next lap anyway, but when more lights on the dashboard started to flicker and the battery voltage dropped to a critical low I knew I was in trouble.

Then, as I started to climb the mountain again, the car cut out. I knew then I had to get this car back to the pits.

I didn't know how I was going to do it, but I had to find a way. I turned the whole thing off for what felt like two minutes, but it was probably only 20 seconds. The other issue I had was that the car was on a slope, halfway up the hill.

I figured I was going to have to roll-start the car in reverse, which is something I'd never done before but it made sense to me during this moment of madness. As I got the car rolling backwards to the point where I had enough speed, I dropped the clutch and the engine kicked in, which then allowed me to just make it to the top of the hill.

All I had to do was get to what we called the grate at the Reid Park section of the track, because from there you could roll the car down to pit lane. While we managed to execute that and get the battery issues sorted, we lost too much time and the race was over. We ended up finishing a lap down in 21st position. Unfortunately for Thommo, we couldn't do the job for him.

There was a bounce back in the next event in Surfers Paradise, then we won both races at Symmons Plains in Tasmania before capturing victory in the penultimate event at Sandown.

Twelve months earlier James Courtney had won that race and it had turned out to be the defining moment of our battle, so I was determined to make it mine this year. The victory meant I went to the final weekend in Sydney with a 188-point lead over Lowndesy.

The scenario was I had to finish fourth or better in the opening race, or just finish ahead of my teammate, to claim my third drivers' championship. As is often the case with these things, that script didn't play out as I touched a wall, damaging the front of the car.

While I was dealing with that my Triple Eight teammate seized the moment and claimed the win, which raised the stakes for the final event on Sunday. My lead had been slashed but thankfully I was able to keep out of trouble, and my eighth place in the last race – Lowndesy ran second – was enough to take the crown with 35 points to spare.

It was a great feeling given how much the circumstances behind the 2010 miss had burned. Dad had driven up from Melbourne to be there and it was awesome to share this moment with him – although there was something different.

I didn't say anything initially and he'd then driven back down to Corowa. When I touched base with him the following day things started to get real, and not in a good way.

CRAIG LOWNDES

Seven-time Bathurst 1000 Champion

Three-time Supercars Champion

Triple Eight teammate, 2006–2018

'You always keep an eye on the next generation, or the newcomers coming through, and Jamie was obviously one of them. The interesting thing is we basically grew up a suburb apart. We raced in the same go-kart club, but it was eight or nine years' difference, so we never really crossed paths in the early days, but we both came through the same programs.

'Roland [Dane] had no secrets in the reason why he first got Jamie involved. It was to partner up with me for the Bathurst rounds, and then when Jamie came on the scene he had the raw speed – there was no doubt about that. There were just some inconsistencies at the beginning that everyone has. I do remember back in the early days he was very much a sponge – learning and developing and understanding. Even I was getting comments from people saying, "Don't tell him too much, keep it to yourself", but that's not me, and credit to Jamie he utilised that throughout his career.

'We are very similar in the sense of our driving style, but we approach things very differently. He reminds me a lot of Mark Skaife in a lot of ways: the dedication into the data, working out every nth degree, sitting in front of the laptop until 10pm at night, trying to extract the best out of himself. But he also works to see where he needs to improve. Whereas for myself, I would look at data, get the download and come out and talk to fans. We were different in our approach but very similar in our style.

'In the early stages I think the teamwork worked really well. He was the up-and-comer. I was the established driver, and then there was that crossover period where he became Jamie. He was his own person, and then he became the thorn in my side. I think I was second to him three or four times in the championship. For me, we always had a very healthy rivalry. Whenever he went a tenth faster, I would want to go a tenth faster than him, and vice versa. The first things that we both used to ask was what each other's lap times were and how we compared.

'In saying that, Roland did a very good job of managing – not the ego – but the expectations of both of us, and we also worked very hard together because we recognised if we didn't work together we would be fighting against each other and we would run midfield instead of one and two. That was very much the philosophy, even today with Shane [van Gisbergen] and Jamie: you work together and it's then on any given weekend whoever gets it right wins. You would rather be fighting for first and second than eighth and ninth.

'It's a credit to Roland in the way he conducted the team; in a sense we are all one. We work as one. If someone has a problem with a car, the other side of the garage comes across and helps out. Again, that philosophy and mentality within Triple Eight over the years is that we all work as a team. Even to the point where when we went to a three-car team, we were the same. I wasn't side-by-side to either Shane or Jamie, but we all worked as one collective group to get the best results for the team.

'Jamie had done a couple of Bathursts before he joined us, so he sort of understood the pressure and the magnitude of what Bathurst brings as an event. I think his maturity over those couple of years was really important, and he had the speed. Like every young driver, you want to lead the first lap, the second lap, the third lap, the fourth lap. He recognised, again, that he had good people around him to keep his feet on the ground, to basically understand that his role was to bring the car back in a good position and let me run to the finish. He did that in 2006. I believe he probably didn't fully understand the magnitude of that year because of the passing of Peter [Brock] and my relationship with Peter, and why it meant so much for me to be on that top step.

'I remember the second year we managed to win it, it was like, "Wow – we can set the record again." A team of drivers had only three-peated twice before. In the third year, Jamie wanted to step up and have more of an established role. He qualified the car and it was great to see. I think that was the crossover period between his enthusiasm and his belief – his ability to believe in himself. He stepped up a massive amount. He was definitely maturing as a person, and it's always been very interesting. If you ask Jamie what's more important to him, a championship or a Bathurst, it is always a championship. For me, it has always been Bathurst. We've always sort of had different individual goals over a season, and I think there is no doubt why he has seven championships while I see Bathurst as the Holy Grail.

'We only crashed into each other once, in Tasmania. At the end of the back straight, I was leading, Jamie was second. I half-left the door open, he had a dive in there, we had contact. He went on to win the race and I got pushed wide, off the track, although I did get going again. We finished the race – I think I was seventh or something – but we potentially could have had a one-two finish. That was the worst one. Roland dragged us into the transporter and gave us a talking to.

At that point Red Bull were very conscious of teammate contact – that was just the philosophy and rules Red Bull wanted us to live by. We'd broken them, Roland was upset, we learned from it, and we never did it again.

'While Jamie had the personality of a Mark Skaife because he was so dedicated to his craft – the driving, the data, the routines – it was also the politics. He loved getting into the nitty-gritty, track safety; everything and anything behind the scenes Jamie would want to know about it and try and fix it, the same as Skaife. The one bad thing for both of them was the accessibility from the public in the early days. I think he learned as the years went on; he got a chance to embrace the sport as a whole, and part of that is the fans. It was just a mindset that he had; there is never a right or wrong reason for any of it. Many guys who I've seen over the past decades have been the same. Marcos Ambrose was the same as Jamie – focused on driving. You have got people like that who focus purely on their craft. There is no right or wrong; everyone has got a different personality.

'Jamie was always pushing himself. The fire within everyone has to come from your own beliefs and pushing yourself. He had that. He was always scrutinising his fitness, nutrition, the data. There is no doubt he has a process. Whether you agree or disagree with it, that's how he operates, or what he needs to do to operate. And it worked for him. Every year you win a championship, you think you are going to win the next one by doing the same thing, but you won't. He always looked at how he could better himself.

'He is getting better at the politics. He definitely didn't have a filter early on; he basically said what he wanted and didn't care what people thought. Which is good on one side, but as he has got older he has mellowed out more – he's embraced it. He has really enjoyed the sport for what it has given him as much as what he has taken out of it, and he probably appreciates it more now, later in life and his career, than when he first started. Again, with every young person, when they start they need to establish themselves, and he worked extremely hard, especially having that 12 months with Garry Rogers. Then Garry basically throws him to the curb, saying he won't achieve anything. I think he had a bee under his bonnet to prove him wrong.'

5

FAMILY

WHEN someone comes up to me and starts complaining about a member of their family, going on about how much they dislike them, I struggle to listen. I can't get past the fact that you need to do whatever you can to look after your family and to be there for them.

I regret not being a better son and a better brother. That's one thing I emphasise when I speak to younger people, explaining the regret I feel and the hope I have that my experiences would sink in for them, leading to a change in their mentality.

Most of us spend so much time with family that they are the first people who get under our skin and annoy us. They're the ones we fight with first, and I'm sure some of the things you say and the way you treat your family on certain occasions, you wouldn't treat your worst enemy like that.

Many think it's appropriate to act badly to family because they'll most likely always forgive you. But what you need to think about is the heartache you put your family through. They are the last people you should do that to.

The one thing my parents taught my sister Sally and me was that good things happen to good people. Dad would often say: 'There are only two types of people in this world, good people and not-so-good people.'

He had a theory that he called the shopping trolley scenario. There are two choices with the shopping trolley: put it back or just leave it out.

When you grab a shopping trolley and take it to your car to unpack the groceries, there's no obligation for you to put the trolley back in the rack. It's not illegal to just leave it next to your car and you won't be fined if you do.

The only reason you would return that trolley is so somebody else won't have to pick it up and put it away for you. That simple act is out of the goodness of your heart to try and make someone else's life easier.

So, according to my father, the good people in this world put the trolley back and the people who don't give a shit about anybody else leave the trolley out in the middle of the car park.

They may try to justify it by saying the big corporations who own the supermarkets have plenty of money and can afford to employ people to pick up the trolleys. That's how they think, and making someone else's day harder than it should be doesn't even register.

Mum and Dad made sure when we were kids that we were always polite to people, used our manners and respected the elderly. They would be horrified if they found out we got on a train and took the last seat away from an elderly person.

We were taught good morals and, most important of all . . . we put the trolley back in the rack.

'Dad, you don't look well. You really have to start looking after yourself.'

I was worried.

My father had just told me how he'd been forced to stop halfway on the journey from Sydney to Corowa because he was starting to feel dizzy.

'It was really weird,' he explained. 'I had to hold myself up on a pole but I then came good. And I had no dramas after that.'

But I knew something wasn't right. He looked noticeably different to the person I saw a month earlier in November.

In typical Dad fashion he was trying to deflect any concerns. He figured once he got to Corowa and breathed in the good clean fresh air he'd come good.

He'd been spending a lot of time at the caravan park to work on his passion project, which was to build a cabin on the site. This cabin had become his big thing in retirement and he was the type of person who was busier after retirement than when he was working.

Corowa really was his perfect place.

He'd picked the spot by the river when there was nothing else around in what was then a brand-new caravan park. It was just a patch of clay dirt that he put the caravan on and from that moment, it had been known as the Whincups' spot.

Dad worked on that spot until that uneven patch of clay dirt was perfectly level with manicured grass, had a paved path and an outdoor dining setting. It was the stand-out site in a park that is now always overflowing with campers and caravans.

This was Dad's castle and he'd worked hard throughout his life, sometimes working three jobs at a time, to save enough money so he could enjoy his retirement.

He wasn't interested in the big overseas trip. He just wanted enough to live comfortably at home, where he could take Mum out to dinner a couple of times a week and then head to the cabin by the river for long weekends and holidays.

Building it himself was typical Dad. He had no qualified trades (actually, he might have, but they weren't the building type) but was big on common sense. He would get out there and have a crack at anything, and if he needed any help he'd ring up one of his mates who was a builder or an electrician and pick their brain.

He'd then apply that into the construction and if he had any issues he'd just get on the phone and find someone who could solve the problem. He'd tinkered away at the cabin for ages and the finished product was pretty impressive with three bedrooms and a decent sized kitchen at the front.

By the time we all got there in late December 2011, Dad was not well. He was really struggling to get out of bed and when he did it was only for a few hours. He'd just sit around and then say he was feeling crook, so he'd go back to bed to try and recover. But he never came good.

It was sad because he used to love getting the family together in his favourite spot and it was always a very important time for him.

The problem was he'd never really looked after himself. Health wasn't a priority.

If you met his mum, you'd understand where his love of food came from. My grandmother was around during the Second World War and her theory was: 'The ones who survived the war had a little bit extra on them.'

So her boy was going to have that little bit extra and Dad used to go around to my nan's house every day for lunch. She lived near his printing press in Preston and would have a three-course meal – soup, the main dish and sponge cake – waiting for him. When I worked there and became part of the ritual, I quickly learned to settle for a toasted sandwich and lay off the cake, as I was trying to fit into a racecar.

Dad never did any training, but at the same time he was as strong as an ox. I'll never forget the few times we had to labour all day. I thought I was fit, but we would smash it out at the same pace. I would drink eight litres of water during the day and end up dehydrated; he would have a cup of tea for morning and afternoon tea. I would be sore and fatigued the next day; he would get up and be good to do it all again. While he didn't mind a beer or glass of wine, I never saw him drunk.

We'd taken him to the doctor a couple of times up in Corowa, but soon realised he had to go back to Melbourne for some expert diagnosis. A stomach ulcer had been identified as a problem, but more extensive testing found out something that rocked all of us.

Dad had lymphoma cancer.

He immediately underwent chemotherapy, but there was a number of other issues at play. And then suddenly everything got worse.

There was the ulcer, blood pressure issues linked to his heart, a problem with an artery in his leg and then internal bleeding, which put pressure on the brain.

It was a rollercoaster that was moving way too fast for the doctors to keep up with and by the middle of January Dad was a shadow of himself.

I'd returned to Queensland to get prepared for the new season, but at the start of February I flew back down as things took another turn for the worse.

Dad was in hospital and could no longer look after himself. Mum had to do everything for him. Not being the man of the family or in control of his own body finally broke him.

It was almost like his brain had switched off and he no longer had any fight left.

On 26 February, 2012, I lost my dad. He was only 66.

But Dad wasn't just Dad to me – he was my best mate.

He'd been with me every step of the way, from buying me my first go-kart when I was seven years old to being by my side when I raised the Supercars Championship trophy.

His larger-than-life presence was always appreciated in the motorsport paddock and he'd often take up the role as chief sausage cooker on the barbecue at the team garage. Dad wasn't one of these fathers who got in the way; he fitted in because he had car racing in his blood. He was an old-fashioned racer.

What I didn't appreciate until it was too late was the fact he'd sacrificed his life for me to succeed. He dedicated his life to making me a better person and a professional racecar driver.

He was a hard taskmaster and a perfectionist. I could've just won a go-kart national championship or a V8 Supercars race at Winton and he'd find something that hadn't quite been right.

You'd struggle to get a compliment out of him. I'd come back after a win and he'd say: 'You lost a spot at the start, what happened there?'

I'd never really had to deal with death in my life until Dad's passing, and to lose a parent and someone who was also your best friend was a grief I struggled to comprehend.

A natural response was to reflect on your life with them – just thinking about our family dynamic always made me smile.

Mum was the perfect partner for Dad and the rock behind all of us. She spent her life trying to make sure everyone else was happy, that everyone was enjoying themselves and being looked after.

She was an absolute pro at having a good time and not being too stressed about anything. Her philosophy in life and what she always told me was: 'Do what you want to do, and if you're happy, I'm happy.'

I'm actually surprised how domesticated I am given I did nothing in my first 20 years. It's embarrassing how little I did around the house when I was younger. Washing clothes, making school lunches, delivering amazing dinners – Mum never missed a beat, ever.

Something that surprised many people was Mum's knowledge of motorsport. She had intently followed my career and was always reading the latest motor racing magazines. There are times where we'd be sitting around and someone would come over and ask a question about Supercars and she'd fire off the answer before anyone else.

That didn't translate into her own driving skills, though. One of my favourite stories about my mum involved a sky blue 1981 VH Commodore, which was my grandfather's car until he got too old to drive. It was actually my first car, but before I took it over when I turned 18 there was a crossover period where it was used as the backup if the main family car was getting serviced.

The thing is, it didn't idle well. It used to stall when it was stopped. Mum hated this and couldn't get her head around it. It was an automatic and all she had to do was hold the throttle down and keep the revs up when she was at the traffic lights. Instead, she would slow down and roll into red lights rather than ever coming to a stop.

This proved to be a dilemma for school pick-up. There'd be hundreds of kids standing on the hill waiting to see their parents' car before dashing down and getting in. Mum would slowly appear in the Commodore but then wouldn't stop, so we'd have to run beside the car, throw our school bags in and then get into this moving vehicle.

Understandably, my sister, who at the time was 16, an age when you were trying desperately to be cool, was always blowing up at Mum about making her look silly in front of her friends. I found it highly amusing.

That was quite a common theme through our childhood, my sister Sally and I not seeing eye-to-eye. We used to fight like cats and dogs over who got to sit in the front seat. Usually that would result in her pulling me out by my collar.

In our teenage years we really didn't like each other, which is pretty much par for the course for siblings going through that adolescent phase. That completely changed when we both matured and ventured out into the real world.

I feel in some way she got the raw end of the deal, because a lot of the family money had been spent on my career through go-karts and Formula Ford. There wasn't much else to go around and there was a few memorable blow-ups where she would rail against Dad, when he suggested we all needed to tighten our spending habits.

Telling Sally, who had long hair past her shoulders, about how to use less shampoo in the shower to save money didn't go down well. Dad got given a lesson in exactly what is required to keep hair of that length healthy.

Sally became a dental nurse and has worked at the same place forever. In many ways, she was a lot more conservative than me and ended up marrying her high-school sweetheart, Benn Minihan. I got off to an interesting start with him.

She'd invited him and a few friends over to have a swim in our backyard pool. I was a bit of a fat kid back then, so when I jumped in the pool they were like: 'Whoa, tidal wave.'

I quickly realised they were making fun of my weight. Luckily I had a massive thick skin even then and brushed it off, but it was a lasting memory and not exactly an ideal first impression of my future brother-in-law Benn. Nowadays we're great mates. I was very proud to be his best man at their wedding, and the way he looks after my mother as he does – really, anyone who helps with their mother-in-law as much – deserves a medal in my books.

We now get on famously and they have two beautiful kids, Mitchell and Chelsea, who I love hanging out with in Corowa, where we teach them how to waterski and we play plenty of one-on-one basketball.

They both have an entrepreneurial streak in them, which I admire.

Every year the kids go around to all of the campsites collecting bottles because they got 10 cents for each one down the road at the recycling depot. They each end up making $250 over the Christmas period. Chelsea also has another side gig, a hair and beauty business, which she also runs at the caravan park, offering $5 massage and $4 manicures.

These are great times – but now one important piece of my family is missing.

Six days was the gap between Dad passing and the opening race of the 2012 season at the Clipsal 500 in Adelaide.

I'd spent the past two weeks going in and out of hospital, which was hardly normal preparation. Triple Eight were amazing, telling me to take whatever time I needed.

I knew Dad would've wanted me to race, and when I boarded the plane for Adelaide I was determined to do the right thing by my teammates and get the job done.

The car felt incredible straight away and we qualified in fifth position on the grid.

Apart from the moment where there was a minute's silence before the race for someone else – I couldn't believe the timing – I managed to keep everything together.

My last line in the pre-race media conference had explained everything: 'He was my best mate. He was the best dad in the world.'

It's very rare when the driver and car feel as one. We obviously spend so much time chasing this nirvana, but there always seems to be something, it could be the tiniest thing, which means it's not quite perfect.

From the start of this race the car felt unbelievable, it was so fast and we had a rhythm going. A big crash early in the race took out some of the main contenders, with Lowndesy taking the lead.

It was shortly after this that Dutto and I made one of the best decisions of our partnership. In 250km races like the Clipsal, teams operate on either a two-stop or three-stop strategy.

Two pit stops in this race meant taking a punt with your fuel calculations, which will give you an advantage through the middle of the race, potentially helping you clear out in the lead. However, it also can result in a more conservative finish given your tyres are old and your eyes are fixated on the fuel gauge, hoping the data is right and you don't run out.

Going in an extra time obviously costs positions on the track during the race, but it does give you an opportunity to make up significant ground in the later stages considering you're on better tyres with no fuel concerns.

Our calculated risk was to go with the three stops, which meant that when I emerged from pit lane with 12 laps remaining I'd fallen back into seventh position.

What happened next was something that is hard to explain. With each lap I was getting faster and faster, dropping lap record after lap record. It was becoming more and more clear that it wasn't just me in the car that day.

As I mentioned, I'm not spiritual at all, but there was something going on, given what was happening over the final laps of this race. Dad was a crazy competitive bugger, which is why I felt he was riding shotgun with me.

The last thing he would've wanted was for me to get emotional – there would be time for that later, but right now I had business to take care of.

That business involved chasing down my best mate Will Davison, who was leading the Clipsal 500. But I was running out of time and laps.

It was going to be tight but I was flying. One by one I was taking down cars. That bizarre sense of purpose I'd been feeling throughout the drive was getting more heightened.

With three laps remaining I was back to second and in Davo's mirror. The gap was down to five seconds.

He was clearly trying to conserve fuel and was slowing as a result. I'd been in his situation many times before and all you could do was pray that you made it to the end.

As we started the final lap I was closing in quickly onto the back of Davo's Ford. But there was still a gap. I knew I had the car. I just needed an opening.

Then it happened.

On turn eight I noticed something had changed with Davo's car. It was the fuel. He was in trouble. As we approached turn nine I dived down on the inside and my mate didn't fight it.

His car was gone.

Davo could have made that pass a lot more difficult to execute but he, better than anyone, understood my situation and for that I would forever be in his debt.

It just confirmed to me that we were seemingly all part of a script that had been written for this day. As I came around the final bend and saw the chequered flag ahead, it finally got me.

A tear formed.

We did it, Dad.

I had lost my safety net.

After getting through the Clipsal weekend and then Dad's funeral on Tuesday – I was required to speak, which was by far the hardest thing I've ever had to do in my entire life – the reality of losing my mentor started to sink in.

All the big decisions in my life, I'd just ring Dad and get an answer. Sometimes he might not have been sure of his answer, but I needed the surety of the call. Just bouncing something off him would help every time and then I'd go out and make it happen.

Losing that safety net meant all of a sudden I had this feeling that I was now required to be the man of the family. I had this overwhelming sense of responsibility towards my mother and sister – not that they needed to be looked after – and felt I needed to step up and start making real life decisions.

I was no longer the kid who was Dave's son. I was the one who had to make things happen.

The first major change in my new mindset was to leave the management company I was currently with. I wanted to run my own show off the track, and the first thing I did was go into the local real estate agent and sign a lease on an office, not far from where I lived in Hope Island.

I needed a home for Whincup Motor Sport Pty Ltd and I also needed a personal assistant, so I put an ad on SEEK even though I wasn't totally sure what I was doing.

The successful applicant was named Samantha, and I'm sure my welcoming address clearly summed up where I was at. 'I don't really know what I'm doing and I don't really have any jobs for you at this stage but I need my life sorted out,' I said.

Fixing my diary, organising flights and sponsorship obligations was a good starting point but basically just being at the end of the phone when I wasn't sure about something was going to be the most important role of Whincup Motor Sport's first employee.

Given the emotional backdrop to 2012, it was appropriate that my co-driver for Bathurst was Paul Dumbrell, one of my best friends from back home in Melbourne.

I'd met PD through Davo, they'd gone to school together, when we were all into go-karts. He soon became our designated driver because he managed to find a way back then to get his P-plates early in Queensland, as his parents had a house in the Sunshine State.

We didn't waste much time on the semantics of this little rort he'd managed to pull because it meant for two years he was our ride.

After school PD would come out and get me because I was at the wrong end of town in the 'Bronx' of Greensborough compared to Will and him, who lived in the glitzy Kew and Balwyn area.

His father, Garry, was a former racecar driver and the man behind the Autobarn franchise, so there was always the odd nice new car in the Dumbrell driveway, which we could often take for a spin.

Us kids owe a lot to Garry. He was always providing us the opportunity to be kids and experience life to the fullest. I will never forget the day we were all in the spa at his house, drinking and listening to music, and he came out with a few more Bacardi Breezers. Walking off, he noticed the 240-volt power lead for the stereo dangling in the pool. He just shook his head, smiled, and said, 'Pretty classy fellas.' He will be missed.

We were young and silly, and on one particularly memorable night in South Yarra we got into some trouble. PD, Davo, another mate Stewart McColl and I were cruising the famous Chapel Street strip on our way to get baby-back ribs at TGI Fridays in a new Nissan 200SX.

It had been raining and PD decided to give the Nissan some stick over the tramline, but the car dipped out, then overcorrected and flew across the road and belted into a car coming the other way.

I was in the back left-hand side of the car and the impact was right there. I could see what was about to happen, so

I covered my head and dived down into the middle of the seats and braced for impact.

Despite being ready for the crash, we were all still thrown around the car and I hit my head on the pillar. What struck me instantly about it was how different it was to being involved in a heavy hit in a racecar.

Obviously in racecars you're fully secured with a proper seat, harness and helmet, but the impact in the normal car was 100 times harder. Luckily I escaped with just a couple of bumps, but Stewie hit his head and got concussed which saw him spend the night in hospital.

It was a low moment for all of us, but at the same time a really big life experience and a reminder of how important it was to take it easy on the road.

While that wasn't one of them, there were plenty of good times with PD, particularly at his crazy house parties where there were lots of Bacardi Breezers consumed around the spa.

The three of us were inseparable, and Tuesday nights were always big as it was uni night at the local pub. Often I'd borrow a pair of PD's flash Diesel shoes for the night given he had plenty of them in his wardrobe, so I always figured he wouldn't miss the odd pair.

We were also very competitive with each other but PD certainly had the bragging rights early, considering he made history by becoming the youngest V8 Supercars driver when he debuted at Symmons Plains in Tasmania in the winter of 1999, a week before his 17th birthday.

It was crazy to think one of my mates was driving a Supercar before I even had my learner's permit.

He then had his first Bathurst 1000 start as a 17-year-old in 1999, where he raced a Wynns/Faulkner Racing No. 96 Holden VS Commodore with Matthew White, qualifying the car in 33rd position before unfortunately crashing out after 11 laps.

Talk about being thrown into the fire, but watching what he went through probably helped me get my head around things when it was my turn for a shot at the big time a few years later.

PD never missed a start in Australia's Great Race after his debut and had finished fifth twice previously.

It was an exciting moment when Triple Eight signed him for the endurance races, as it gave two mates the chance to do something they'd dreamt about as pimple-faced kids digging it up on the go-kart tracks of Melbourne.

We had a strategy meeting in the hire car during the three-hour trip from Sydney Airport to Bathurst and mapped out what we thought would be the best driver strategy. PD and I were pretty chuffed and thinking we were engineering gurus when we presented this piece of paper with letters scribbled all over it to Dutto.

He was actually quite welcoming as he'd come up with something similar, but more importantly the garage presented the No.1 Holden Commodore in brilliant shape once again.

Not that it needed any more hype than usual, given it stood alone as the jewel in the Supercars crown – but 2012 marked the 50th anniversary of Bathurst.

And we were up to our eyeballs in it from the start after qualifying in second spot on the grid. The key to Bathurst is making sure you're still around and in contention when the clock ticks over the six-hour mark.

Pushing too early can lead to mistakes, so being clean and getting your strategy right is the priority. Ironically we found ourselves in the direct opposite position to the Clipsal 500 race in Adelaide seven months earlier.

This time we were the ones who were going to be running on empty at the end of the race. We had the lead, but over the final stages my attention was on two things – the fuel gauge and David Reynolds, whose Ford was closing rapidly.

The data wasn't kind reading. Generally a V8 Supercar uses approximately four kilos of fuel for each lap at Bathurst and we only had 59 kilos with 15 laps remaining. We were one short.

This meant I had to find a way to conserve one kilo of fuel while also trying to hold out Reynolds, which made it a classic case of cat and mouse.

Throw into the mix the fact my tyres were starting to go and it was game on for the final lap.

Reynolds was all over me and there were certain parts of the track where I knew I could slow down because he couldn't pass. It was heart-in-mouth stuff, and as I approached the final turn there was still a sense the engine could surge at any time.

Thankfully that didn't happen and after 161 laps there was just 0.313 seconds between first and second.

For the fourth time I was the Bathurst champion, but it was the first time I'd actually driven the final leg to the chequered flag. This meant a lot, but not as much as people probably thought as I'd always figured the co-driver's role in these endurance races was invaluable and should never be downplayed.

After a quick burnout in front of the Triple Eight crew I made my way slowly around to the presentation area. As I got out of the car, the photographers were there waiting for the money shot of the winning driver climbing onto the bonnet and celebrating.

But I waited.

Something was missing. I wasn't going to get up on that car without my mate PD next to me.

It's what Dad would have done.

PAUL DUMBRELL

Two-time Dunlop Super2 Series Champion

Co-driver, endurance races

2012 Bathurst winner

'My story was I went to Xavier College, and a guy named Will Davison was in my same year. I didn't know Will from a bar of soap, to be honest, but we were both travelling up to Queensland to spend school holidays with our families, and a mutual friend said we should catch up and go to Wet 'n' Wild – or whatever you do when you're 10 years old. So our families caught up, and my dad said, "I know Will's dad, Richard," so we became friends. Will was already racing go-karts, and I started racing go-karts, and then Will, Jamie and I became good friends. We would have been 13 or 14, and since then, the rest is history.

'There were some good go-karters back then – "Frosty" Winterbottom; James Courtney was a couple of years older than us but was coming through roughly at the same time. It was very rare that a whole generation came through together. It was a little bit like what has happened in V8s over the last couple of years: there were no retirements for a number of years, and then all of a sudden four or five happen at the one time, and that really changes everything.

'I was 17 when I got my licence up in Queensland, which was good. That probably cemented our friendship – maybe it was slave labour if I look back on it now. I was the designated taxi driver for many years. I started in Supercars in '03 and Jamie started in '04. We qualified on the back row of the grid a few times, so we looked at each other in 23rd and 24th. I was with Larry Perkins for three or four years and then moved around a bit before landing at Triple Eight for seven or eight years.

'Jamie and I did seven or eight Bathursts together, and I think there was only one where we didn't have a chance to win. We were either leading or in the top two or three going into the last hour. Jamie and I said all the way through: we would drive to Bathurst every year and we would talk about strategy for three hours on that drive. And it was pretty much the same conversation seven years running in the end, and all we said was, "Let's just get ourselves to that last hour, don't take risks, the race is not won in the first hour." That was always how we thought, let's put ourselves forward for the best opportunity and outside of that one year we literally had as equal a chance as anyone else. We had some good fortune, some bad fortune, we zigged left when we had to zag right, but it's just the history of the race. A legend like Glenn Seton never won the race, which is a travesty for people who deserved that right for all they had done for the sport.

'Bathurst in 2012, that was the year Jamie's dad died, so it was really emotional for many people for many reasons. Outside childbirth and getting married, Bathurst is next. What we joke about afterwards is how we will be telling our grandkids about those two best mates who stood on top of the podium in one of the biggest races of the year. It was the 50th anniversary as well – there were a number of good milestones there – and even better, Jamie stole the car from me as well. He ended up buying the car before I could.

'We were coming off Sandown, where we'd been one of the quickest cars but were passed late in the race and finished third, so we went to Bathurst really wanting to make amends. J-Dub and my approach to that race, being our first year, and every one after that, was: it's about the last 10 or 20 laps of the race. There is so much media, emotion and commotion, and probably, to be honest, after that year we were the lead talking point – from things going wrong or going against us or making mistakes, which we all did at the time.

'We just wanted to put our heads down, and that race played out like a number of them afterwards, in terms of our feel for the strategy. It was a nerve-racking moment. I can't remember how many laps we had to go, but we obviously knew the inside story in the team about how tight or tough it was going to be. Roland [Dane] came over with three or four laps to go and said, 'We're not going to make it; we've got to pit to protect the championship'. But J-Dub had different plans and managed to bring it home. That famous old saying about "half a can of juice", well, that's all he had left out there, and fast-forward a few years later, and it was half a can short.

'There were a lot of Bathurst races up until that stage that had been won hours earlier with a 20 second lead. This was a very different emotion. We didn't know we were going to win until we literally came across the line. Jamie could have come out of the last corner and ran out of fuel and got passed. Just that sheer emotion was there. Everything Jamie must have been thinking about, the exhilaration he would have been juggling, and the exhaustion of the race.

'We were up cheering as a team on the other end of pit lane, and we then had to get down to the winner's rostrum. Jamie refused to stand on the car until I got down there, and I don't think I've seen any other driver do that. We were minutes away from reaching him, not 10 seconds away, where he could see. He was asking the media, "Where is the team? Where is PD?" That just explains the person Jamie is – it's not about individual accolades, it's actually about the team and making sure everyone who is a part of the success is there. I mean, you get to the end and you're drained, you just go through the motions, you get directed – do this, do that – and you sort of go through the motions. But he made that conscious decision to wait for me. It was my first Bathurst win; but regardless of that, it was a sign of the value he put on the whole team effort on that day. It was about getting the whole team there.

'When I reflect back, it was sometimes a tough drive home on a Monday morning or Sunday night. I don't have any regrets. A lot of people say Jamie did this or we did this or the team did this, but you win and lose as one. You take the good with the bad. Sport is a calculated risk. Sometimes people don't talk about the calculated risks when they go well – they just talk about the win. In the 2012 Bathurst we did win, we took the risk; we could have easily pitted to protect the championship and not won the race.

'Then in 2014, we ran out of fuel. Since when at Bathurst has there been a red flag? It was lunchtime and we were sitting in the motorhome eating a banana, and we were saying the only time you do this at Bathurst is when you've crashed. That set off a chain of events with fuel forecasting, the track breaking away, all those types of things. It was the first time anyone had gone through that.

'After the race we headed home. We jumped into the rental car and got the fuel forecast – now, my numbers could be wrong, but say it was 300 kilometres to Sydney Airport, and we had 290 kilometres of fuel on the dash – we looked at each other and said, "Let's do it." We rolled into Sydney Airport with zero kilometres on the fuel gauge. We were about to put it on social media but we refrained, thinking it might have been a little bit raw at that time. You have to look at it like, you roll the dice and sometimes it comes your way and sometimes it doesn't.

'The thing about Jamie is his sheer determination and willingness to go the extra mile. There are plenty of stories of Will and I waiting at dinner for him, or what not, and he has decided to stay back with the team. This is when we were racing in different teams. He would stay back and do an extra debrief, and he might have neglected to tell us that he wasn't coming. At the end of the day, he was put on this world to win car races, just with his dedication and sheer understanding.

'I knew him as a friend for 15 years before I became his teammate or co-driver for those last few years, and his drive was an eye-opener to me. He is a perfectionist, which sometimes drives frustration. I probably didn't understand. It was in his pursuit of ergonomics, just the feel of the game. Absolutely everything to do with his approach was second to none, and I think that approach is actually more common practice today.

When we were going through the fitness training, his dedication was far from the standard. Jamie set that standard for what the sport is today.

'I think what gets written about Jamie or spoken about Jamie publicly, and the Jamie that Will or I or any of his friends know, are polar opposites, but everyone is entitled to their opinion as well. I put it down to a number of things, some Jamie-orientated, some generational. Craig [Lowndes] was taught by Peter Brock, and both are fan-friendly people. Jamie took a different approach. He looks at it as perfection on the track, and if you have delivered perfection on the track then that should speak volumes to the team, the sponsors and the fans. I think he also speaks his mind as well, and that can be polarising. He said it like it was – and maybe sometimes too much – but that's how it is, and that's what makes him who he is. And there was definitely some tall poppy syndrome. There was definitely a run there of four or five years where he would win 50 per cent of the races. Triple Eight and Lowndesy were dominating as well, and in every sport there needs to be a villain, and that was Jamie.

'When we were teammates, we had some very frank conversations with each other. I knew all he wanted to do was make me better, and it was a two-way street. Maybe that is why we were good teammates; we actually cared. I didn't want a full-time drive, from the day I stepped out of full-time driving I never wanted a full-time drive. All I wanted was to help him win, and I've said that many times over the years. If we finished fourth in every single endurance race but that enabled him to win the championship, then that was what I was there to support. Of course I would love the endurance race wins, but many co-drivers have come to try and audition, and that's where plenty of challenges present themselves.

'Roland and Jamie will probably hate me for saying this, but they have many similar traits – very different personalities – but it's in their competitiveness and willingness for perfection. Some of his worst races are some of his biggest wins, because he says we could have done better.'

6

CAR V. DRIVER

IT'S an age-old debate in motorsport that has kept fans and experts divided for generations: Does a perfectly engineered car make a driver? Or is it the talent of the driver who can make a car perform better?

This was quickly becoming a discussion point centred around Triple Eight after my 2021 championship victory (Lowndesy finished second). I'd now won four of the past V8 Supercars titles and finished second in the other.

There were plenty who were in the car camp. According to them, the only reason I was winning was because Triple Eight had proven to be the best garage on pit lane with the best machinery, the best mechanics and the best engineers. In fact, there were even suggestions that the genius of my engineer Mark Dutton was the entire reason behind our success.

We took it as a compliment in many ways because I understood that I was an important cog in a very big wheel, which included everyone in the Triple Eight garage.

This debate had raged in Formula 1 over recent times when assessing the careers of two greats in the sport, Michael Schumacher and Lewis Hamilton.

Schumacher had won a couple of championships with Benetton before he went to Ferrari, who at that stage had been struggling for years. 'The Prancing Horse' went on to win five championships in a row. Was it him or the car?

Hamilton equalled Schumacher's championship record of seven in 2020, and it almost took that for people to recognise that it wasn't just the car but his driving talent that had a fair bit to do with his success.

Good teams breed success. They work together to form an environment that can give their drivers a mentality of invincibility that can then be translated onto the track.

This had happened to me. I'd reached a point in my career where I felt that I was the best driver in the country. That may come across as arrogant, but I didn't care – I knew that nobody could drive a Supercar as well as I did.

But there was always an asterisk in the minds of many, although a change in 2013 was going to give me the perfect opportunity to prove a point once and for all.

'You don't have to win every fight, you've just got to win the war, and that's what the year's all about.'

The cameras were rolling at the launch of the 2013 season and the game, not just in the Triple Eight garage but all across the Supercars community, was about change. It had been talked about for a while and the moment had finally arrived: the 'Car of the Future' project was becoming a reality.

There was a whole new war about to break out with the biggest shift in the sport in decades happening in the new season.

The aim was to even the playing field by introducing new rules around the build and design of the cars. Essentially, we were all going to have the same cars. They were going to be lighter, more economical, have increased agility and be more competitive across the board, which therefore created better racing.

This also opened up the Ford v. Holden battleground to other manufacturers, with Nissan and Mercedes-Benz joining the championship.

On top of all that, Triple Eight had signed one of the biggest sponsorship deals in Australian motorsport with Red Bull as the replacement for Vodafone, who were stepping away from the sport.

For the launch I was posing in front of my new Red Bull-backed VF Commodore V8 and I felt strangely excited. This was the change I desperately needed.

I'd hit 30 years of age and having just won my fourth drivers' championship I'd allowed my mind to wonder about what was next. There was a precedent with Marcos Ambrose having dominated Supercars and then making the move in 2006 over to the States to race NASCAR.

That was something I knew I could explore, which I explained to the assembled media who seemed taken aback that I'd consider anything new given my current dominance.

'Everyone takes my answer a different way, twists it, turns it,' I explained. 'But without a doubt: if we were running last year's car this year, I'd have to be looking at something else.

'Don't get me wrong, I've got one of the best jobs in the world. But it just goes to show that no matter how good your environment is, if you keep doing the same thing, it becomes repetitive.

'I was hoping for a breath of fresh air. I've hit the reset button, I really have. In my mind I feel like I'm the new kid on the block who hasn't won anything. It sounds pretty stupid, but that's my mentality.

'I feel like I'm in a new category right now, with the feel of the car and the change.'

A lot of the new adjustments sounded small and technical but they dramatically altered the feel of the car.

One of the major advantages we'd enjoyed at Triple Eight was on the engineering side, and that was being stripped back. The areas of the car you could play with had been reduced to ensure everyone on the grid was a match.

For example the smaller, lighter roll cage was a massive change. This was previously an area where we'd have an engineer on a computer for three months just dedicated to finding ways to have the best weight-efficient roll cage, because lightening and lowering weight while maintaining rigidity throughout the car was the whole name of the game from a design perspective.

There was a minimum weight each car had to hit, but the lighter you can build the structure of the car, the more lead you can put along the bottom. That's where you want the weight, as low as it can be, rather than having weight everywhere.

Other changes included the glass windscreen being replaced with polycarbonate, the engine had been moved back 100mm, and the fuel cell was placed in front of the rear axle. It was now fitted with a transaxle gearbox and differential, which was supported with independent rear suspension.

There was an upgrade to 18-inch wheels, which meant lower profile tyres and bigger brakes.

And the biggest kicker for the authorities' plan to even the playing field was the reduction in costs with these new generation cars. The average V8 Supercar cost around $600,000 – the 2013 Car of the Future model was closer to $350,000.

The changes had certainly created a buzz around pit lane ahead of the start of the season, although I nearly wasn't part of it – and it had nothing to do with my NASCAR dream.

I'd found myself in the middle of a bitter dispute between our new team sponsor Red Bull and one of my own personal sponsors, rival drink company Monster Energy.

Since 2009 I'd displayed Monster Energy on my helmet as drivers were allowed to have their own individual sponsors around the team's main backer. When RD told me about the prospect of Red Bull coming on board, I understood I had to get out of the final year of my contract with Monster because it was an obvious clash.

However, Monster weren't accommodating and I effectively became a pawn in a far bigger fight. I believe they saw the helmet issue as a way of trying to keep Red Bull out of Supercars.

It got to the point where they threatened to put a restraining order on me from racing for Red Bull with the very real prospect that I might have to sit out the season.

Monster weren't seeking specific damages, it seemed; they just wanted to mess with us. Part of that was stopping me from doing any promotion for Red Bull, which wasn't an option in anyone's eyes at Triple Eight. Not having the reigning champion able to promote his team's new major sponsor was ridiculous.

The legal stoush ended up in the NSW Supreme Court for a three-day hearing, where I was required to give evidence. It was a daunting experience and eye-opening on many fronts.

As a result of the legal proceedings I started the season with a neutral helmet – which was a throwback to when I first started.

There was one bonus: I certainly walked away knowing a lot about contract law. From that point forward I'd be a lot more careful with the wording in my deals. In the future there would always be the clause that states any personal sponsorship wouldn't be allowed to conflict with a team sponsor.

It was an awkward way to start an exciting new partnership with Red Bull, who quickly showed how they were head and shoulders above most others.

Instead of just being a big cheque and a few stickers on the car, they were more concerned about how they could make us a better team. They sat us all down and wanted to know how the operation worked, warts and all. In particular, they wanted to know what our biggest hurdles were.

One thing that continued to haunt us was our poor history of reading the weather. It seemed that every time the weather played a part in a race, we struggled to figure out what tyres we should put on.

So what did Red Bull do? They went and hired us a weatherman to be on track with us, providing up-to-the-minute expert analysis of what was happening in the heavens.

After the dust eventually settled on the legal dispute I managed to get my own personal helmet sponsorship with Red Bull, which was a dream for me given their focus was making me better as an athlete, rather than how many PR events I could do for them.

We were the perfect match.

While the new car took a lot of getting used to, we managed to get it right on one of the most important weeks of the year.

For the first time V8 Supercars raced in the United States at the Circuit of the Americas in Austin, Texas. It was marketed as the 'Aussie Invasion' with four 100km races split over two days and almost 70,000 motorsport fans checking us out.

The biggest thing we had to deal with was the heat. The temperature was hovering around 32-degrees Celsius, which meant the inside of the cars was close to 60 degrees.

Adding to the difficulty was the small window between the races. It felt like we literally got out of the car, jumped straight into an ice bath to cool down and then after what felt like five minutes there was a tap on the door to alert us that the cars were going out again for the next race.

We managed to win both races on the Saturday and made it three out of four for the trip by snaring the final race on the

Sunday. It was a great experience and great exposure for both car and driver.

My father taught me very early on that if you're backed into a corner you fight your way out. He was always reminding me that if things get hard you have to step up, go harder and attack.

Sport needs rivalries, and the fans certainly got to see a classic Holden v. Ford showdown again at the 2013 edition of the Bathurst 1000.

And once again I found myself in the middle of it, pitted against my long-time rival Mark 'Frosty' Winterbottom. Our history went way back to the go-kart and Formula Ford days, and the heated battles had continued in Supercars.

We'd had a few scraps over the years where we both gave as good as we got. There was a race back in 2000 at Eastern Creek in the Ford Kart Stars series where he'd touched me off and forced me to crash. In the next race I immediately returned the favour, which led to Frosty and Uncle Graeme exchanging words in the pits.

The relationship had been testy ever since, and it flared again during race seven of the 2013 season at Pukekohe in New Zealand when Frosty tried a reckless move on my inside, which pushed me off onto the grass.

Luckily I was able to avoid disaster, and I actually came back to win the race, but the flagrant attempt to take me out was at the front of my mind for the next day's race. This time Frosty was in the lead and I was second when I did a big dive bomb on his inside, which went astray, sending him off the track with the resultant crash breaking his steering and ruling him out of the race. I was able to continue, but the stewards weren't happy with the incident and hit me with a 25-point penalty.

Why he didn't get any sort of penalty the previous day continued to grate on me afterwards.

We were very different types of people, and the media certainly enjoyed our tit for tat, making it part of the narrative coming into the Great Race.

Paul Dumbrell and I had just won the Sandown 500, which increased my lead in the championship. This confidence flowed onto qualifying where we took out the Top 10 shootout to start from the coveted pole position, with Frosty second on the grid.

It was a promoter's dream that transpired over the next six hours. Frosty got his nose in front after the final compulsory pit stop – there was a new rule that we had to do seven stops in the race to cater for the fuel economy issues of newcomers Nissan and Mercedes-Benz.

So for the final 20 laps it was a one-on-one war. With two laps to go, I really ramped up the pressure and dropped a wheel off the track coming out of the Chase on lap 160 as I contemplated what my plan of attack was going to be.

Now it was down to picking my moment on the final lap. I flicked on my hazard lights, one of the oldest tricks in the book, to try and distract Frosty.

The second turn at Griffins Bend was going to be my moment. The element of surprise was crucial, even if it was for a split second, and as we approached it I faked to go on the inside, then suddenly pulled to the outside and dived hard.

We were alongside each other momentarily and all I needed was Frosty to not be able to hold his line and I was in, because I had the inside running into the next corner. He'd have no choice but to yield.

I got halfway there and for a second I thought he broke early and I was going to do a Craig Lowndes around the outside. I paid the price for the move, sliding wide and losing momentum.

That was the race there.

He now had a small buffer, which barring any monumental mistake, I wasn't going to make up. I got back to almost on his bumper by the final bend but I simply ran out of time. The margin on the finish line was just 0.47 of a second.

It had been a great stoush and these were the moments I lived for – the head-to-head battles. To his credit, Frosty got the upper hand this time.

However, I wasn't feeling as warm and fuzzy about it at the post-race press conference when he made a big deal of slamming down the Peter Brock Trophy in front of me. The moment wasn't lost on the assembled media and it was duly noted by me also, but I knew who'd be having the last laugh.

That came in the final event of the season in Sydney where I became just the fourth driver in history to win five championships.

The battle for the title had been close with Lowndesy and Frosty both having chances to steal it. But victory in the first race on Saturday all but ensured I joined the late Ian

Geoghegan, Dick Johnson and Mark Skaife as the only five-time title winners in Australian touring car history.

All I needed to do in the final race on Sunday was finish among the top 21 finishers, and I did that comfortably, coming in third. For the third straight year Lowndesy came second, so all up it was a great result for Red Bull Racing.

Given the backdrop to the start of the season, the new car and regulations, the legal fight and change going on everywhere, to come out on top gave me huge satisfaction and gave those invested in the car v. driver debate something to think about.

I'd won the war.

A summons to have a sit-down with the boss after winning the championship is normally a very good thing, but this catch-up as we packed up after the final race went in a direction I wasn't expecting.

I'd barely settled in the chair when RD hit me straight between the eyes. 'Dutto is no longer going to be your engineer,' he said.

Luckily I was sitting down – this revelation completely floored me. I was momentarily lost for words. *Why? Why? Why?* pounded through my head.

Dutto and I were the most successful partnership in Supercars history; we'd won more races than any other driver–engineer combination. Why would you want to disrupt that?

RD explained that he was promoting Dutto to team manager, so he would still be around and involved but just not solely focused on what was happening in the No.1 car in 2014.

While I understood the move and was happy for Dutto for being rewarded with a significant promotion, I couldn't shake the anxiety I felt about the situation. We'd had some serious black art going on.

There'd been an understanding between me and Dutto that was off the charts. We didn't have to write things down or have pages of notes to pore over to get things right – we'd just simply have a chat.

We were on the same wavelength and I didn't know if that could be replicated with someone else. But as RD pointed out, for things to get better they have to keep moving forward, and this was an overall team decision that would make us all better.

Dutto's replacement was my data engineer, David Cauchi. He was younger than me and full of passion, enthusiasm and drive. I liked that.

He was the type of person I would select every time. If you gave me the choice of someone who has unbelievable natural ability and skills but doesn't have the right attitude and thinks they're better than everyone else between someone who would work their arse off because it means so much to them, the latter's the guy I want in my corner.

I'm not saying Cauchi didn't have an unbelievable skill set – he did and he was ready for the job – but his passion was his calling card.

As expected, there were teething problems because it was obvious Dutto and I had been fairly slack in regards to reports and documenting things due to our unique understanding. But my new marriage got off on the right foot, winning the opening race of the season in Adelaide and then going on a mid-season run of dominance that gave me a significant lead in the championship.

Another victory with PD at Sandown had us ready to right the wrong of the previous year at Bathurst. That was until qualifying.

In what I can only describe as an amateur mistake, I lost control going up the mountain through the Cutting in qualifying and slammed into the wall, doing significant damage to the front of the Commodore.

We'd been struggling with the set-up at the start of the weekend, and I felt like I'd been too slow through that section of the track, so I pushed it and lost the rear end through the kink.

It was pure driver error and it was our first flying lap because the session had been delayed due to red flags after Ford's David Reynolds had a big crash.

The damage looked worse than it actually was so we were going to have a car ready for the Great Race, the only problem was we'd be starting at the back of the grid.

This led to a lengthy debate inside the garage between Dutto, Cauchi, PD and myself about who would start the race. In recent times most teams have gone with the co-drivers starting the race, but I felt because we were coming from position No. 25 we probably needed a change of strategy.

If we were going to be a factor in this race, we had to do something pretty special early. It was a challenge I embraced.

Once again the guys in the garage had done an amazing job getting the car back up and running and we were quickly into a groove, picking up rivals at a good clip. I actually broke my own lap record on the way to finding the lead by lap 22.

When I handed over to PD a few stints later the lead was almost half a lap, but unfortunately the race soon came to a standstill after Luke Youlden's Holden hit a kangaroo that had jumped onto the track. This wasn't an unusual situation; there were hundreds of kangaroos who lived on Mount Panorama and they gave officials sleepless nights.

But things were about to get even more bizarre after some resurfacing work, which had been done on the track at Griffins Bend leading into the weekend, started to open up and resulted in three crashes. The stewards stopped the race and it was the first time in history that a red flag didn't end the race, since there hadn't been enough laps to determine a winner.

The delay allowed teams to make running repairs to damaged cars or change parts that had proven suspect in the early laps – perfectly in line with the rule book – which made many in pit lane upset with cries of an unfair advantage.

I was oblivious to it all because I knew the break was going to be at least an hour, so I went back to the Red Bull motorhome and had a sleep. Bathurst is such a massive week that you have to take advantage of any opportunity for some downtime. I had to actually be woken up by one of the team for the race restart.

It was clearly going to be a crazy day, and on the first lap of the restart I had a scrap with Todd Kelly's Nissan, which saw me heading back into the pits with tyre damage after spinning out. To add salt to the wound, the stewards also hit me with a drive-through penalty, which meant we went from the lead to being a lap and three-quarters down.

That generally means your day is done. But this was no normal day.

Somehow with five laps remaining we found ourselves back in the lead. A fortuitous safety car had helped the situation, but it was incredible that we were going to steal the Great Race. There was no way we should've been in this position given where we'd started and what had already transpired.

We'd taken a punt to get into the lead by staying out while everyone else pitted. The problem was this meant we weren't sure if we had enough fuel to get to the end.

Throughout the day we'd never actually run the car into the reserve tank because we kept pitting before it got there. There's no fuel gauge in the car – all the car does is measure how much fuel is going into the engine and doesn't display how much is actually in the tank.

But once you hit the reserve tank you basically know it's nearly empty and you can reset your calculations. The issue was because we'd been continually filling it up, we weren't 100 per cent sure how much fuel was in the car.

The team was telling me to conserve fuel and I had a number I had to hit for each lap. When you crossed the finish line after the completion of each lap the number would come up, which tells you how much fuel you've used.

On average I was doing that. Some laps were better than others, but overall I felt I was doing a good job considering

I was juggling tyres and also trying to keep the lead in the race from Ford's Chaz Mostert, who was closing in fast.

It was a very similar scenario to 2012. We'd got it right then and I was confident we could do it again now. All I had to do was get to the two-lap mark before the reserve tank kicked in.

Unfortunately, with two-and-a-half laps to go, a light on the dashboard flicked on. I was instantly gripped by fear.

The reserve tank was now being used. I wasn't going to make it.

We needed a miracle so I backed it right off and managed to hold Chaz up as much as I possibly could, but as we started the final lap I knew it was only a matter of time.

Then as we headed into Conrod Straight the car coughed. I was gone. Chaz saw it and made his move, which I could no longer counter, and from there it was a matter of just praying we got to the finish line.

In the end I rolled there because, as predicted, we did run out of petrol. Three other cars managed to pass me in that short amount of time, but as I slowly made my way to the garage I was overwhelmed by a sense of pride.

That was one of the best races I'd ever been involved in, and I was so proud of the team for continuing to fight despite all sorts of obstacles. To take a lead into the final lap and to even finish fifth was nothing short of extraordinary.

The team, and in particular RD, weren't expecting the big smile I had on my face when I got out of the car.

'Fellas, I can't ask for any more,' I said. 'That is one of the best team efforts I have ever seen.'

The comment went down like a lead balloon; it was obvious they were all fuming about letting slip this golden opportunity.

There was a sense I'd pushed the car too hard and didn't save fuel when I could have, which I didn't believe was right. That debate would go on, but for now I was more focused on what an incredible job everyone had done in what was one of the more bizarre races in Bathurst's long history.

I was proud of the team's effort and I saw it as one of the best performances during my time at Triple Eight.

In the post-race interview I repeated those sentiments, which I soon realised was like poking the bear for RD. The more I showed how happy I was with the performance, the angrier he got.

He was clearly looking for someone's head, and I was the easy target. I expected a belting behind closed doors but he was so riled up that he made his feelings known in public.

'Jamie has won us a few races over time, but this one he lost it for us,' was my boss's assessment of Bathurst 2014.

In the big picture debate, his thoughts were clear: Car 1. Driver 0.

DAVID CAUCHI

Triple Eight Race Engineer, 2014–2021

'I think if you look in any sport, Jamie's kind of dominance, for that long, is pretty unheard of. It is very, very rare. Fundamentally, why has he been able to do that? Obviously, he is very dedicated to what he does. From a young age Jamie worked hard at his craft. He has been able to maintain that dedication, that drive to continuously improve himself and the car. He understands that with motor racing it's man and machine and the team around you. You need all those things working for you to be successful.

'He's managed to not only continue to improve himself and rise to the challenge of different drivers and different teams that have popped up over the years and challenged Jamie and Triple Eight, but he always manages to find *another* level any time that happens. He hasn't waved the white flag or given up. I think that's the thing that stands out the most: he has this real ability to always look for the next improvement, the next thing we can do better as a team and with the car. He's always analysing himself as well.

'It is also an industry where it can be quite easy to blame other things. You can blame the car, you can blame the engineer, you can blame the mechanics – the excuse book is very, very long, but he knows that he is the key part of that very big wheel. Fundamentally, he is the one who has to win, and sometimes it's not happening because of another part of the wheel, because the engineers aren't doing a good enough job or the team is not doing a good enough job – but he is fundamentally a big part of that. He can't just wipe his hands of it and walk away and say, "That's not my problem." He is really ingrained in the entire motor sport machine.

'The uniqueness of motor sport – I guess it is like any individual sport – is, when it comes down to it, it's Jamie and the car against 26 other drivers. It's down to him and his ability on the track. Obviously there are still elements where the team has an influence on the end result – pit stops, strategy and all those kind of things – but when you're watching it and you see those guys, *they're* the ones in the cabin. It's a hard job. You watch it on TV and it looks like they're cruising around for a Sunday drive. I can assure you, they're not. They are absolutely on the limit. I will never forget, and it was only a recent event, watching Jamie and

Shane [van Gisbergen] get out of their cars at Townsville after a 250km race. They had no reason to be going as fast as they were, but they were absolutely belting each other right until the very end, and that just sticks in my mind as a pure show of how dedicated and how hard these guys are pushing inside these cars.

'As an engineer, you have to have an understanding of what they are going through. Individual sports can be lonely, and you can go through a range of emotions in the car, especially if something has gone wrong or something hasn't gone your way. Sometimes, even when you're out in front and are lucky enough to be in that position, it is so hard to maintain your focus. The smallest mistake in these cars can mean going off the circuit and losing seconds or having a crash, so the consequences for a small mistake are actually very, very big.

'It is up to the engineer to then understand what the driver is going through at different phases of the race, what information he needs when you need to talk to him, when you need to be encouraging him, and when you need to shut up and let him do his job. Those are the things you learn over time. Jamie is a great guy, and I think now people understand him better. Over the years he has been one of the most misunderstood people. I am great friends with him off the track, and you couldn't meet a guy who is more relaxed and friendly. He definitely keeps his personal life personal, as his professional side is obviously very public. He is so easy to get along with, and I think we have very similar overall values and views on life and motorsport. It's worked really well, and he's been a pleasure to team up with all these years. The relationship between engineer and driver doesn't always click, but I can definitely say it did between Jamie and me, and it has been a pretty fun journey.

'We are all different animals. We all have different personality traits, but I think sometimes Jamie had a much harder time than he deserved. When you are a professional and the one performing at a very high level like Jamie has over a long period of time, you just have to accept that there are going to be haters out there. There will be people trying to bring you down instead of lift you up, and I think that is just a part of professional sport, whether you like it or not. That's just one thing that you have to overcome, because you can let that kind of thing affect you mentally, which can then eventually affect your performance on the track.

'That is also a very big part of looking at Jamie overall and why he has been so successful – he's been able to separate himself from all that kind of stuff and not let it affect him in the car. I can only think of a handful of times, if ever, where I feel like he was affected by something someone might have said or by something that happened, whatever it might be. When he gets in the car, I have never seen him influenced by any of the carry-on.

'That's another thing that I really love about Jamie – he's always pushing the limits inside the car and pushing us to the limit as well. Sometimes that doesn't pay off, and you have to accept that, but if he just drove around conservatively all the time we wouldn't have had the results that we have had. Sometimes pushing the limits has cost us. We've absolutely lost races because we took some risks that didn't pay off, but it has paid off for us a lot more times than it hasn't. If you play conservative all the time, you're not going to achieve the results you're after. It's easy to not push the limits and just roll around in 10th.

'If you look back at almost any spectacular race over the last few years, you could almost guarantee that Jamie would feature somewhere – for the right or the wrong reasons – and 2014 Bathurst is the perfect example. We'd crashed in qualifying. I remember standing underneath the bridge as we were second-last on the grid. That first stint in the race we said, "Right, you have to start the race from back there." He brought the car back – I'm sure it was inside the top 10. That stint was unbelievable, and then we had a number of issues. We hit the wall and thought we'd damaged the suspension, so he came in and pitted, but it was just a flat tyre and he we went out again. We were up the front, then back, then up and back again, and in the end we took the risk on fuel and it didn't pay off. But it will probably go down as one of the best races in the history of that event for a very long time.

'That day there were a lot of things that didn't go our way from inside the garage and inside the car. We needed a little bit of luck, all those little one percenters we were on the wrong side of. We had some inaccuracies in our calculations, which were a little bit out – we used a little bit too much fuel in certain phases of the race where we should have saved a little bit more. We got those 50–50 calls inside and outside the car wrong. That day we just weren't meant to win the race.

'2017 for me, personally, was the year I am still the most proud of. We had the rise of DJR Team Penske, the Scott McLaughlin era, and those guys were really coming. We knew they were going to be a big force. We knew Scotty was a talented driver, and it was literally a matter of when and how long it was going to take for them to be a force. That year we were developing the ZB Commodore in the background. At that point we were still racing the VF, so from a personal perspective we had a lot going on off the track, outside of just going racing. We were developing this car for next year, so we were having to dedicate a lot of time to that project, which sort of took away improving the current car. The DJR Penske car and Scotty were getting better and better. That year was a grind; of all the years, that was one where we had to really, really dig deep and keep believing in ourselves. I was so proud that we didn't give up until the absolute last lap, and that was eventually how it played out.

'I think some people forget that we actually went into the last round in Newcastle with the championship lead, and we then crashed at turn four on the first lap of the first race on Saturday. Then all of a sudden we weren't leading the championship. We went into the last as a long shot. The old saying of Scotty having one hand on the trophy was true. I remember saying to Jamie, "Mate, this is still on. We're not giving up here, anything can happen." And sure enough it did. Jamie ended up winning that race, with Scotty tangling with Craig [Lowndes] – you couldn't script that kind of thing. It was pretty unbelievable, but basically we never stopped believing that we could win that year. We somehow managed to get it done, and considering the circumstances of that last race and how it all went down, it will be very hard to top those kinds of circumstances and that kind of drama in any other championship win. That will be something I'll never forget, and it was pretty special in the history of the championship.

'Jamie is actually the most chilled-out person I know. For someone who takes a lot on, he is still driving, he has the car wash business, and now he's taking on the management role at Triple Eight. He's got all sorts of things going on, but I never go and see him and say, "Oh my God, Jamie is pulling his hair out." I have never seen him in that state, and I am quite jealous of it because one of my weaknesses is I don't actually know how to switch off. I struggle to relax. I think that is a side of him that he has taught me – you need to be able to actually turn off, as that makes you better when you are switched on.

'One of our funniest moments came in New Zealand in 2019 when Jamie passed the safety car. We had spoken about it before the weekend in the debrief. I'd said to him, "Look, here is a place where they can stuff up the safety car." We had got done by it once before, and that stuck in my head and in his head, so I told him before the race, "I'll make it very clear if you come out of the pits and you're not the leader. I will tell you that you are not the leader so don't lose time, because we will lose positions if you lose any time behind the safety car." And sure enough it happened. We had been leading the race, then the safety car came out. We pitted at that point and then weren't the leader when the safety car was on the circuit with yellow lights. I was on the radio telling him, "Do not lose time behind the safety car, you are not the leader, make sure you don't lose any time." He was like, "You were screaming at me and I felt if I lost any time you were going to be pissed off at me, so I went past the safety car."

'While we were gutted, as we should have won that race, we still had the ability afterwards to have a laugh and accept that we both played a role in what had happened. It's stuff like that: his ability to have a go, to put it all out on the track and then, win or lose, sit back afterwards and have a bit of a laugh about it. Don't get me wrong, there are plenty of times after a race when we haven't laughed, but at the end of day he has the ability to put it all back in perspective and have a bit of fun, even when things go against us.

'Jamie heading into management is going to be great for Triple Eight. RD has done a very good job for a very long time – the results speak for themselves – but this will be a different sort of fresh spark. He will bring a whole new energy to the place, and he will be without doubt one of the most highly criticised team principals because of the history of the team. But I think he is very used to that over his career, so I don't think that is going to be anything new to him.'

7
LOVE THE GRIND

ONE of the things I'm most proud of is my longevity.

Being able to avoid the burn-out syndrome that has claimed many over the journey is one of the tougher parts of the gig. It takes a special mentality to keep fronting up year after year and ticking off those one percenters that make the difference.

To do that, you have to love the grind, and in the competitive motorsport arena if you don't have the grinding mentality then you're going to be spat out pretty quickly. It is really something that you have to learn to love. There is nothing glamorous about the late nights at the workshop, poring over data on your laptop followed by the early-morning alarm at 5am to go running or riding to keep the body strong.

Everything is focused on getting the car ready for race day, finding that new part or new way of going quicker while also preparing yourself mentally and physically to go into battle.

And then when that race is over, you do it all again the next week. The same thing, the same grind.

But like everything, there are always ups and downs, as I was about to find out.

It might sound strange but I'd never really thought about the number six.

When you're in the heat of the battle, and then obviously remaining in it, there's a tendency to think numbers are just numbers. And that's all.

By winning the 2014 title in the second-last event at Phillip Island, I knew I'd created history and become the only driver to win six V8 Supercars Championships.

A tear was shed when I crossed the finish line to win the second race at the Island, which gave me an unassailable lead. I didn't even have to turn up to the season finale in Sydney to claim the crown. But, as I always say, you're only as good as your last race, and the grind waits for no-one.

So when the calendar ticked over to 2015 the alarm was still going off at dawn for my morning run, and the shopping trolley was still full of the healthiest foods in the supermarket.

I'd become borderline obsessive about health and fitness as my career had gone on. There were a few reasons for this, starting with the Whincup fat genes.

As I've mentioned earlier my grandmother was probably to blame for this given she loved feeding the family, and I always joked there weren't too many skinny Whincups walking around.

Sometimes I felt if I looked at the wrong food for too long I'd put on weight. It took me almost 10 years of training six days a week to feel like I had a handle on things, and I needed to work really hard to get down to my race weight, which is around 76kg.

A driver's weight used to be a priority, as there was no minimum weight limit – the lighter you were the less weight you are braking, cornering and accelerating around the circuit. These days there is a minimum driver weight of 103.5kg, but this also includes all your racing gear, racing seat including mounts and seat insert, plus all the leg protection in the footwell. I'm well under this limit, so I have to run lead ballast under my seat to get me to the 103.5kg. While there is a small centre of gravity advantage to being light, the main motivation to keep the body fat levels down is so I don't need to pump as much oxygen around my body when working hard behind the wheel.

You are what you eat has become a mantra I live by. I've been able to see a direct connection between what goes into my body and how I prepare mentally and physically to drive a Supercar.

To become a better racecar driver, a good starting point is to spend more time honing your skills. Generally the people who excel at something are the ones who spend more time on that activity than anybody else. But to be able to spend that time and be more dedicated you have to be fit, feel good and have a clear mind.

In my case, it all starts with the diet. If you're feeding your body the right food, it's going to give you that motivation to get started, get out of bed, get moving and get those hours in.

If you think of a pyramid, diet is at the top for me. Then you work your way back from there. If you don't get that right then the rest, such as achieving greatness, is all the more difficult.

It's a proven fact that as an athlete the more knowledge you have about nutrition the better. But what blows my mind is how little most of us know about how our body works and the fuel it requires.

One of the biggest issues in the world is the fact that more people die of heart disease and poor general health as a result of bad diets than anything else. Yet it feels like the focus is often elsewhere, with a lot of time and money spent chasing solutions for other diseases that don't do as much damage.

Many people feed their pets better than they feed themselves. Most dog owners would make sure their pets are eating the healthiest dog food, yet at the same time they'll fill their body with rubbish every day and not be concerned about it.

They're cutting years off their life and setting themselves up to go through all sorts of medical issues because of poor nutrition. Too many people are frying their brain on alcohol, drugs and a bad diet, which is having a negative impact on society.

It's a major issue but in my own little world I know what works for me. It's not uncommon to have to excuse myself from team events, as the food offering isn't quite up to competition spec, and I find myself down at the local Woolies buying organic chicken and spinach leaves.

Putting the right fuel in your body makes the training so much easier, although that's probably not a word to describe a Supercars driver's fitness program.

The physical stress to drive one of these cars is significant and our training is based along the same lines as triathletes, incorporating long-distance running, riding and swimming.

A regular week of training would involve a 2km swim in the pool, a couple of 8km runs, followed by time in the gym with a trainer. There is a 60km bike ride in the middle of the week while the weekend involves a 10km run on Saturday and a 60km ride again on Sunday.

Throw in some go-karting as often as possible, which sharpens up the driving skills and is a good physical workout. A spin on the mountain bike and kite surfing are also part of the regime.

An insight into what our bodies go through on race day explains why health and fitness is so important. In an endurance race, like a 250km event, I'd sweat out seven litres of fluid in a two-hour stint, considering I'm operating in a confined space and wearing multiple layers of clothing in 50-degree heat.

It's seriously hot, and during that time I'd drink four litres of water, which meant that when I stepped out of that car I'd be 3kg lighter than when I started (given that a litre of water comes to one kilo). Getting the fluid back in before the next day's race is important, so a lot of the post-race focus is on rehydrating.

We used to get on a drip to accelerate the process but that's no longer allowed. The problem is you'll often find yourself waking up in the middle of the night because your body is screaming out for more water.

It all comes back to one thing: the fitter you are the better you can handle all of these situations that can make or break you on race day.

Unlike other drivers I don't like to focus on my training publicly. In fact, I used to create the opposite image and make out that I was lazy compared to my rivals. It was fairly common to see photos on Instagram of other drivers training, happy to highlight their 100km bike ride. I'd go the other way and give out this vibe that I wasn't too big on training and I just did enough to get through.

I wasn't the fittest out there. Tim Slade, for example, could run 10km in 35 minutes and do a 150km bike ride twice a week. Mark Winterbottom was always pumping us his link to the Essendon Football Club, where he would often train.

Those guys were probably fitter than me, but I always thought that overall, when you combined all facets and looked at time dedicated to the sport, I was in front of everyone else.

There is obviously a physical component and a skills component in being a V8 Supercars driver, because you need to have good car control, but really it's no different to any other sport in that to succeed you need to be mentally tough.

And, just as important, you have to be able to grind it out.

I didn't believe in omens until I met Fluffy.

Fluffy was a black-headed python I became acquainted with at Taronga Zoo as part of the official launch of the

2015 Supercars season. The idea was to have some drivers mingling with the animals, which some PR genius thought would make for great pictures.

We fed the giraffes, but then they wanted to make things interesting and unveiled Fluffy. I'm not one of those people who's worried about snakes – I see them as fairly harmless creatures.

So they put Fluffy around my shoulders. Usually the snakes are uninterested and don't really do much, but this time was different. She kept turning quite strongly, trying to get to my hand, which I later figured out still had food on it – or the smell of food – from when we fed the giraffes.

Fluffy was clearly agitated, so after a few quick photos I happily gave her back to the handler. However one photographer, who was either late or hadn't got the shot they wanted, requested that we do it again.

I wasn't impressed but thought it was best to do the right thing, so they put Fluffy back on my shoulders. This time I was nervously watching her every move. And then it happened. In the blink of an eye Fluffy latched onto my hand, biting right onto my knuckle, around the thumb area.

The handler quickly got her off my shoulders, but Fluffy wasn't releasing from my hand. He didn't want to rip her head away because the snake's teeth are angled backwards, which meant I would've ended up with snapped teeth embedded in my hand.

I remained surprisingly calm, while the photographers and TV cameras sensed they were onto something good and were snapping away, almost with glee. The handler got hold of a drink bottle and tried to force water down the snake's throat, but Fluffy refused to release her grip.

His next theory was that the snake might be stuck, so he asked me to unclench my fist and slowly raise it in the air. But when I did that Fluffy reacted by trying to swallow my whole hand.

By this stage, I was no longer seeing the funny side of things and we started twisting the snake's head firmly sideways. Eventually she let go and they managed to secure her in a bag, but there was blood pouring from the wound.

They quickly took me to the on-site medical centre, where a doctor gave me a tetanus shot. The Taronga Zoo staff were very apologetic about the Fluffy incident, and I had a bit of a laugh afterwards, but it was certainly an interesting way to start 2015.

Unfortunately, it set the tone for the season.

While I continued my love affair with the Clipsal 500 and took out the opening race of the season in Adelaide, it was all downhill from there. I went through one of the biggest dry spells of my career, going 12 races without a podium finish.

There was a combination of reasons, some of which I have to put my hand up for, but there was no doubt the strength of the competition had increased. No longer was it just Triple Eight and Ford Performance Racing sharing the races between us – everyone in pit lane had stepped up.

Without this shift the sport was in danger of plateauing, so while I could see the big picture, and understand the benefits to the sport, I wasn't comfortable with what was

Playing in the mud at the Hume Weir Caravan Park, Albury, 1987.

Testing my brand-new Suzuki 50 at home in Greensborough, 1986.

Helping Uncle Graeme service his V8.

The race team all ready to go, Numurkah, 1992.

First go-kart podium trophy. I took 2nd place at the Swan Hill Club Day, 1992.

First go-kart trophy, Driver of the Day, Brooklyn, 1992.

Barefooting on the Murray River, 1995.

Debuting my new Tecno/Parilla kart with Dad and Peter 'Topsi' Temopoulos, Eastern Creek, 1999.

Eastern Lions Kart Club, Rookies Champ, 1992, with John Moore (left) and Michael Webb (right).

My first Formula Ford, 'The Red Rabbit', just before I crashed it, Phillip Island, 2000.

Hanging out with (from left) Will Davison, Andrew Gilbert and Mick Ritter at the Australian GP, 2002.

Holding the Formula Ford Championship trophy at the presentation night, with Mum and Dad, 2002.

Time for a quick shot with Davo as I walk back from the Bathurst podium, 2006.

With Dad, celebrating winning the round and being in championship contention, Tasmania, 2007.

It was all smiles at the 2007 Gala Awards, with Roland Dane and Craig Lowndes.

Testing my radio in the McLaren F1 car, Albert Park, 2010.

On a promotional tour of Abu Dhabi with (from left) Will Davison, Paul Dumbrell and Mark Winterbottom, 2010.

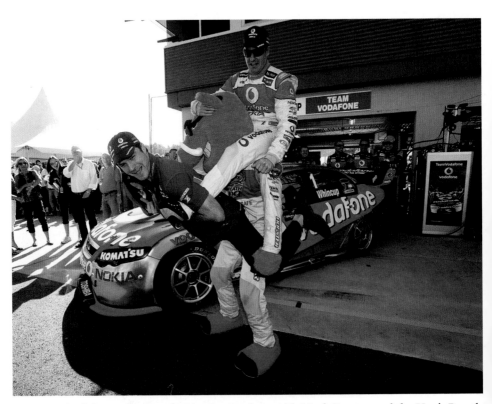

Racing isn't all fun and games, but it sure was here with Mark Dutton and the Hog's Breath Hog at the debut race of the Dunlop Townsville 400 in 2009.

Winning my fourth Bathurst 1000, with Paul Dumbrell, 2012. (Matt Blyth/Getty Images)

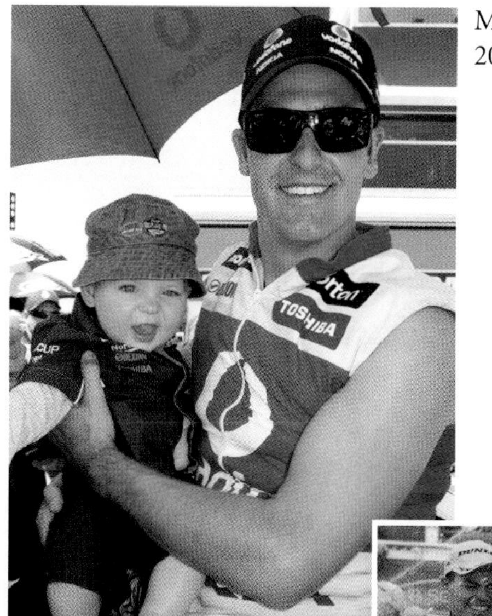

Me and my nephew Mitchell, Phillip Island, 2009.

That's championship title number three in the books, celebrating with Craig Lowndes, 2011. (Mark Horsburgh/ Edge Photographics)

Skydiving with (from left) Steve Johnson, David Reynolds and Will Davison at the Gold Coast, 2012.

Christmas party at Dreamworld with the amazing Washed/LOCA Cafe Crew, 2018.

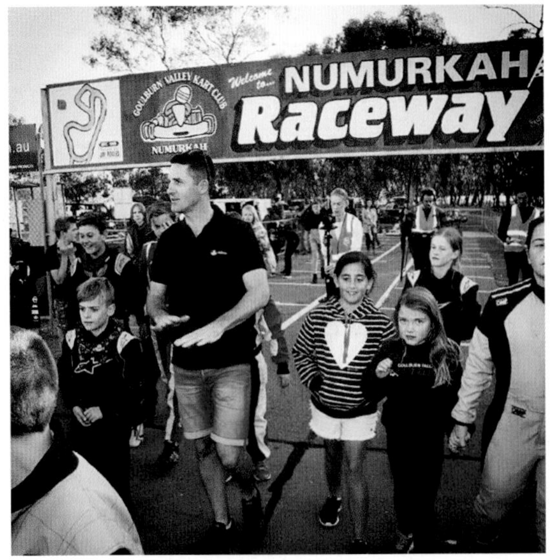

Chatting to the next generation about racing lines, Numurkah Raceway, 2020.

It's always good to shift into the simple life with mates like Davo, Yarrawonga, 2004.

Jetskiing with Paul Dumbrell, Port Phillip Bay, 2004.

North Stradbroke Island getaway with (from left) Jess Dane, David Cauchi, Sam Watts, and Kelly and Tom Wilson.

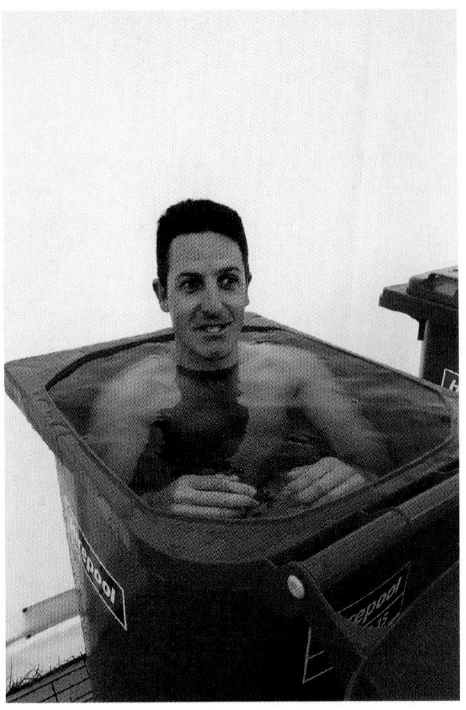

Getting the pre-cooling done without the luxuries, Pukekohe, New Zealand, 2019.

Just before Fluffy tried to eat my hand, Taronga Zoo, 2015.

Pre-season training for the 2017 campaign, Brisbane. (Andy Green/Red Bull Content Pool)

My 100th Supercar win, Eastern Creek, 2016. (VUE Images/Red Bull Content Pool)

Winning my second Jason Richards Memorial Trophy, New Zealand, 2017 – a career highlight, in honour of a great man. (VUE Images/Red Bull Content Pool)

That championship-winning feeling, with David Hadfield and Kris Goos, 2017. (VUE Images/Red Bull Content Pool)

Having a run in the Red Bull Project Sandman wagon with Dan Ricciardo, 2017. (Mark Thompson/Getty Images)

Taking F1 driver Max Verstappen for a spin on home ground, Albert Park, 2019.

Victory at the Gold Coast 600 with Craig Lowndes, 2019. (Daniel Kalisz/ Getty Images)

Living on the edge, Gold Coast, 2019. (VUE Images/Red Bull Content Pool)

The Car1 Crew, Phillip Island, 2014.

Not quick enough in the shoot-out – breaking it down with SVG, Townsville, 2019. (VUE Images/Red Bull Content Pool)

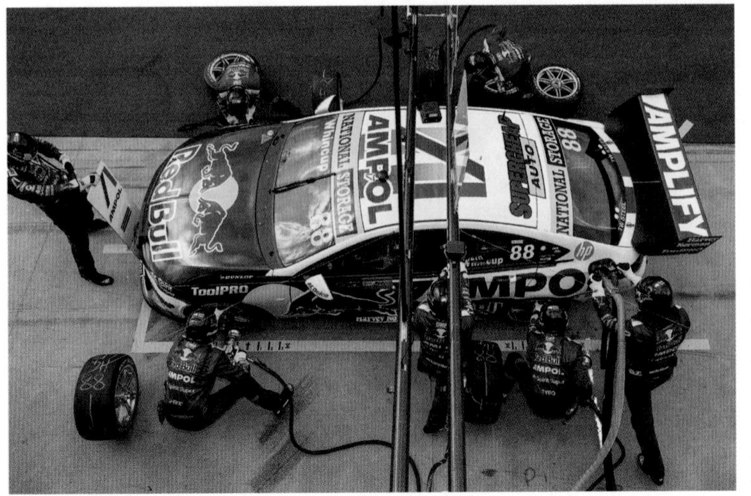

The best crew in the world doing their thing, Bathurst, 2021. (Mark Horsburgh/ Red Bull Content Pool)

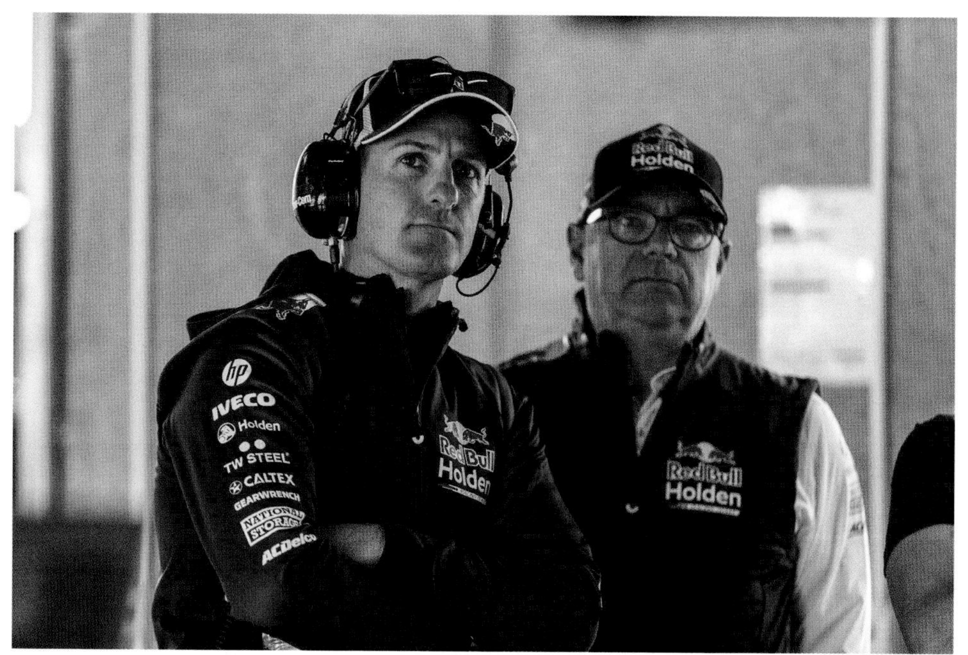

Trying to think like the boss, with Roland Dane, Bathurst, 2019. (VUE Images/Red Bull Content Pool)

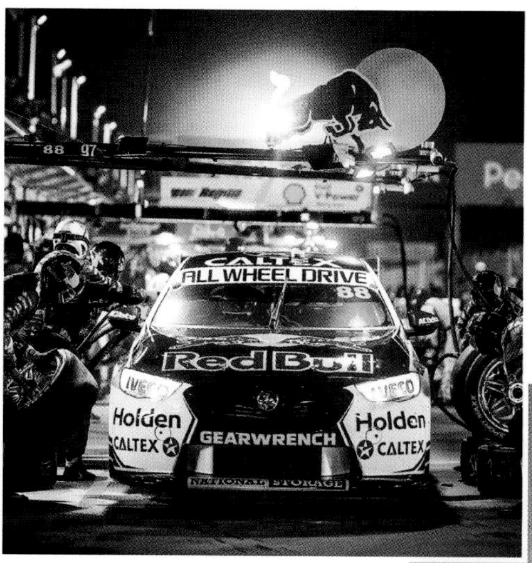

Under the lights at Perth, 2019.

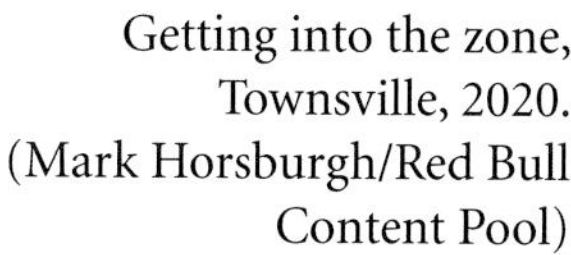

Getting into the zone, Townsville, 2020. (Mark Horsburgh/Red Bull Content Pool)

Listening to Lowndesy on the radio, Bathurst, 2019. (VUE Images/ Red Bull Content Pool)

It was bittersweet to hang up the helmet, but I was excited to welcome Broc Feeney into the team as my replacement for 2022. (Chris Hyde/ Getty Images)

The Townsville Sunset, 2021. (Mark Horsburgh/Red Bull Content Pool)

happening with my team. We'd seemed to take our eye off the ball, and it's always the little things that show you this.

A perfect example came at the Sandown 500 where PD and I had started from pole and were comfortably leading for most of the race when we punctured.

The incident happened on lap 115. Only three laps earlier we'd come in for a scheduled tyre change. We later worked out that a bracket had been dislodged during the pit stop, which caused the rear right tyre to bust.

So we'd gone from having one hand on the trophy, which would've breathed life into my championship run, to battling away to finish 15th.

Ahhh, the little things.

This certainly ramped up the pressure for Bathurst, which was next on the calendar. There was no need for any further motivation, given I was still smarting from running out of petrol 12 months earlier. Our miscalculation had been the story of that race, and once again the Triple Eight No.1 car found itself making headlines for the wrong reasons.

This time it was driver error, but there were different interpretations of it depending on who you are. The bottom line was I passed the safety car, which earned us a drive-through penalty and ruined our chances of winning.

My personal take was that although I knew the race was under safety car conditions, it had green lights flashing when I approached, which is why I kept going. Obviously if I'd seen the safety car with orange flashing lights then I would've stopped.

The team viewed it differently because I'd ignored an instruction to pit and slot in behind my teammate Craig Lowndes under the safety car conditions. Generally that's what we do, but it's not written in stone.

When I saw Lowndesy pull into pit lane I thought the team had made an error. I was under the assumption there was no safety car issue, which is why I stayed out there. It was my call – and a bad one.

The error meant we finished 18th, but after the race I was keen to deflect the controversy as Lowdnesy had gone on to win his sixth Bathurst 1000 with co-driver Steven Richards. It was a fantastic result for the team and I was determined to celebrate the achievement rather than wallow in my own self-pity.

It meant I left Bathurst in eighth spot on the championships table, although there was some saving of face in the final stages of the season where I won five of the last nine races to finish fifth overall.

But it had been a tough year on many fronts.

The search for answers started quickly but I already knew one of them . . . there would be no more promotions involving a snake.

8
ADAPT TO CHANGE

THE ability to change is survival, in life and in motorsport.

Charles Darwin's famous quote (even if he never actually said it) has resonated in recent times: 'It is not the strongest of the species that survives, nor the most intelligent; it is the one most adaptable to change.'

Animals fascinate me, the crocodile in particular, which is a perfect example of adaptation. They have the ability to lower their heart rate to two beats per minute and sit in a mudflat for six months without eating. And then, when required to adapt to a change in circumstances, they can go and ferociously hunt down a fast-moving deer.

The world has thrown many curveballs at us, particularly with COVID; it's changing quickly in so many ways. Whoever can adapt to change the best, whether in sport, business or other areas of life, are the ones who will continue to succeed.

If you see a better way, you have to go down that path and not get stuck. This is something as a racecar driver I have deliberately studied and implemented. For me to remain competitive, I can't just stick to the same driving skills and do the same things I've been doing for the past 10 years. I wouldn't be competitive or winning races anymore.

In a way, I've had to swallow my pride because it's very easy to say, 'I know how this works. This is the way I've won championships in the past, and this is what has given me an edge over my opponents.' If the new kid on the block is doing something differently and I'm pig-headed about resisting it, I'll get left behind.

You can always learn something new, and if a young driver is taking a different line into a corner or has a different technique warming up tyres or drives differently in the wet, I have to be across all of those variables and potentially learn from them. The most important thing is being open to change, because the reality is some of these new techniques are actually better and will help your longevity in the sport.

I'm finding more that if I'm 50–50 about something I'll lean towards jumping in and learning more about that new product or new strategy. In a way, I'm just proving to myself that I can adapt.

It was a scenario I was faced with when a talented New Zealander walked into the Triple Eight garage.

'There is only one rule: we don't run into each other at Triple Eight.'

For the second time in my career I was hearing Roland Dane's warning as he welcomed a new member to the Triple Eight family, Shane van Gisbergen.

An expansion to a three-car team in 2016 was the reason the New Zealander was my new teammate, although it was a bit different to when I'd arrived as a wet-behind-the-ears rookie.

For starters, he was 26 and already had nine years' experience in Supercars. Shane had recently been a part of the one-car Holden TEKNO Autosports team that had punched well and truly above their weight. And he was already one of the best drivers on the grid, finishing runner-up in the Supercars Championships in 2014 and then fourth in 2015.

We had a good precedent with Lowndesy and me being able to help each other, so having another contender under the same roof was only going to lift everyone's performance.

As for RD's golden rule, there had only been one occasion where he'd had to reinforce it.

It was after a messy incident at Symmons Plains in Tasmania in 2014, and it's one I still regret to this day. We were both at fault and it was deemed a racing accident afterwards, but I still felt guilty.

Lowndesy had been in the lead and I'd gone to pass him on the inside but he shut the gate late, and the tangle resulted in my teammate leaving the circuit.

While I'd gone on to win the race it was a hollow victory. RD pulled us both into the trailer and reminded us in very clear terms what he thought about his two drivers bumping into each other. The word 'unacceptable' was used a few times, and the declaration was that if it happened again we'd be looking for new driving arrangements.

In many ways this was the beauty of RD and the reason why he was the most successful – and at times the most hated – team owner in Supercars. Funnily enough, people saw him in probably the same way they saw me: you're either with him or you're not.

RD, who was born in Ireland, has been around the motor industry all his life and started in car sales where, at the height of his powers, he imported Rolls-Royces and Bentleys throughout Asia.

He then dabbled in motorbike racing before switching to racing cars. In 1996 he co-founded Triple Eight Race Engineering in the UK, which was General Motors' factory British Touring Car Championship racing team.

In late 2003, he ventured out to Australia and took over the former Briggs Motor Sport, and so began the transformation into this Supercars Championship powerhouse that now had three legitimate title contenders under the one roof.

The thing I love most about RD is this: at the heart of it all, he's a racer. He loves to win, and he loves to celebrate wins. He sees bringing the team together to enjoy the success as one of his most important tasks, and he'll always be holding court on a Sunday night if Triple Eight has had a good weekend. His go-to is a nice Italian meal with a pretty bad Italian lemon liqueur called limoncello, which I try to steer away from.

What some people don't like to admit is that RD has been an unbelievable asset to Australian motorsport. People don't see on the TV what goes on behind the scenes and the amount of work he does with the Supercars authorities and Motorsport Australia to make sure the sport in this country is as strong as it should be.

While his focus is obviously Triple Eight, there are many decisions RD has made that have benefitted other teams, particularly in terms of pushing sponsors their way. Maybe the recognition will come when he's retired, but there's no doubt in my mind the whole sport owes something to RD for his contribution to ensuring a lot of people make a good living.

One of the most asked questions when it comes to my boss is where did the name Triple Eight come from?

The story goes that he was doing a presentation with his business partner in England, and they quickly needed a name that would fit into a racing context and was also one people would remember. RD had done a lot of business through Asia, especially in Hong Kong and Singapore, where the number eight is a lucky number – and obviously triple eight was three times as lucky.

And now he had a lucky three drivers.

Shane kept up the tradition of Triple Eight newcomers by making a mark early in the 2016 season, finishing third on debut in Adelaide and then winning his first race in Red Bull colours at the next event in Tasmania. It was the start of an epic battle between the three of us that ebbed and flowed throughout the season, with the two endurance events of Sandown and Bathurst having a large bearing on the ultimate result.

And unfortunately we seemed to have developed a magnet for trouble.

At Sandown we made the call to stay out, rather than pit, when there was a safety car, which raised eyebrows before Paul Dumbrell fell afoul of the stewards. They deemed that PD had removed his seatbelt too early in pit lane ahead of a driver change, and the resultant penalty pushed us back to 12th.

Shane finished second and in the process took a seven-point lead in the championship.

That bitter pill was nothing compared to what transpired at Bathurst, where talk of a curse continued to get more and more momentum.

There was an edge to us that year, and we nailed the practice sessions on our way to winning pole position after the Top 10 shootout. We managed to maintain our place at the pointy end of the race for the opening six hours before things got very interesting with 11 laps remaining.

Scott McLaughlin's Volvo was in the lead, but I was right on his hammer. My confidence was building. I sensed I had the better car underneath me, given we were on different fuel strategies.

His team had elected to stay out and maintain track position, whereas we'd gone for the extra pit stop, which meant I was fuelled up and able to attack the final phase of the race.

It was just a matter of when, not if, I had a crack at him.

Then on lap 150, as we came out of Forrest's Elbow, there was a slight error by McLaughlin, which gave me a great line coming down Conrod Straight. This was my opportunity.

As we came into the Chase he was still a touch wide coming into the bend, so I went for it, dive-bombing through on the inside. I was almost through when my back rear brakes locked up momentarily and there was slight contact, which forced McLaughlin onto the grass.

Although I knew I wasn't at fault for the incident, in a situation like this when there could be doubt in the officials' minds, you're best to redress and make another pass in the following laps.

As I began to slow down to enable my rival back on the circuit, another problem appeared. Garth Tander had been trailing us, and he saw the touch-off as an opportunity to pass both of us. The problem was as I hit the brakes, and he quickly moved to avoid running into the back of me, McLaughlin reappeared at the exact same moment. This created a three-car sandwich with lots of contact, sending cars and debris flying everywhere.

It was a disaster.

Fortunately I escaped relatively unscathed, but my two rivals were in all sorts of trouble, both crashing heavily into the barrier, causing significant damage to their cars.

No-one likes seeing that happen and I felt bad for them, but I saw the incident as just hard racing. The pass was there, I had every right to attempt it, and then what happened on the redress with Tander wasn't my doing.

The stewards didn't agree and my heart sank when their decision came through on the radio: 'A 15-second time penalty for car 88, which will be added to its race time.'

I couldn't believe it. They were ending my race for something that wasn't my fault. It was the wrong call.

All I could do was put my head down and try to put as much space on the field. I already knew we would protest the ruling, but that didn't stop the hollow feeling as I crossed the line first.

As soon as I got out of the car I went and apologised to the McLaughlin and Tander teams, because I was upset about what had happened. But that wasn't an admission of guilt, far from it. It was just the right thing to do.

My version of events was certainly supported in the Triple Eight garage with Dutto and RD already discussing an appeal.

The eventual winner of the race was my good mate Will Davison and Jonathon Webb in their TEKNO Autosports Holden Commodore. There was something out of the wreckage for Triple Eight, with Shane and his co-driver Alexandre Prémat grabbing second.

We did end up appealing the Bathurst result, but nine days later it was dismissed by the Supercars National Court of Appeal, who found we had no grounds for the appeal. It was tough to take, and on top of missing out on another victory in the Great Race, being relegated to 11th place had cost me significantly in the championship.

That magnet of trouble was back at the penultimate event in New Zealand. And this time I was on the wrong side of RD's golden rule.

With the title on the line, Shane and I were duelling for the lead in the third race at Pukekohe when things went astray. He had given me space briefly, and I took the opportunity to pass on the inside, but again I locked the rear brakes and made contact. Shane was spun around onto the grass while I also spun out but remained on the track. It was a bad error and I immediately went to redress it by slowing down until my teammate had got back up and running.

This wasn't enough for the stewards, who again hit me with a drive-through penalty. Thankfully, Shane recovered and ended up finishing third while I limped home with my head down in 25th position.

RD wasn't happy, but I didn't receive the full spray as there was a short turnaround before the fourth and final race. In a clever strategic move I won that one ahead of Shane for a 1-2 Red Bull finish – the best way to calm the boss.

After nine months of battling it out with my new teammate, the championship came down to the final two races in Sydney. I needed Shane to fall over for me to pinch it, but that wasn't how I approached the race. Again, I had to put my head down and do what was right for the team.

And that was to win the race, which I did.

Behind me there were some anxious moments for Shane when on lap nine he had an altercation with Mark Winterbottom, which earned him a drive-through penalty. That pushed him back to 22nd position and, with me in the lead, there was a possibility the championship decider could fall to the following day's race.

But to his credit Shane showed all of his champion qualities, seizing on a perfectly timed safety car to then charge through the pack for the miracle finish, which got him next to me on the podium in third place.

That was enough to secure the title, which was a defining moment – not just for Shane and Triple Eight, but for my outlook.

Change had happened, and I had to adapt.

I have never been a big drinker, but a social beer around the barbecue with friends and family is something I've certainly enjoyed. It's an Aussie tradition, and I've loved nothing more than a bit of beach cricket with a few cold beers.

Not anymore.

I came to the realisation that some major sacrifices had to be made if I was to keep up with the next generation, who'd fired a clear warning shot with Shane's 2016 victory.

There was a seven-year age gap between us, and given I was turning 34 a month before the start of the new season, that made it an 11-year difference back to my other main rival, Ford's Scott McLaughlin.

My entire focus had to be on winning that championship trophy. Alcohol was gone and I wasn't hanging out with friends as much. I had my tunnel vision locked in. Everything was being dedicated to preparing to drive. My training and attention to detail on the diet went to a whole new level. In the garage I was working overtime with my engineer David Cauchi to make the car perfect.

The results weren't there immediately but car No. 88 was consistently on the podium; in fact, we were there nine times before finally getting our first win for the year in Townsville.

Shane had started well, winning the opening three races of the 2017 season, but midway through the year it was apparent McLaughlin was going to be the thorn in my side. As usual the double points for the endurance events were going to make or break the championship.

A pile-up on the opening lap saw the red flag out for a major delay at Sandown, where PD was starting the race. After the resumption he soon found himself in the lead, only for a tyre puncture to spin us out of contention. We did manage to complete the race and scramble to sixth, but with McLaughlin finishing second it meant he took an 84-point lead into Bathurst.

The trek to the mountain was bringing with it an extra layer now, with the inevitable talk of a hoodoo given the recent goings-on in the Great Race. We did our best to ignore it, just tried to tick all the preparation boxes on the expectation that at some stage there'd be some love from the motor-racing gods.

The gods certainly did have a say in the race, with the heavens opening for the first time for the whole week right before the start of the race on Sunday. And this wasn't a passing shower. There was heavy rain with even some fog thrown in. The conditions were treacherous, and the focus for the first part of the race was to simply stay out of trouble and stay on the track.

We couldn't work out how to stop the front windows from fogging up. We had run in the wet before and applied the same strategies. We'd tried to fix it with extra air vents and sealing the car to keep the water out, but nothing seemed to work. We needed to do something quickly, as it was going to stop our race . . . so we rolled out the hand squeegee. We literally had a stick in the car with a sponge and rag set-up on the end, so when we were on the straight we could try and rub the fog off the screen in between gears. (As expected, after the race the idea was instantly banned from a safety point of view. Weeks later, back at the workshop during the full R&D mission to try and find a fix, we read the fine print on the Rain-X we were using, and the bottle read 'Upholstery Cleaner'. We were bloody using upholstery cleaner as anti-fog.)

Despite the dramas, we found ourselves in the top five as the race neared its crucial final phase, when out of nowhere the hoodoo struck again.

I couldn't believe it. On lap 119 I heard something pop in the engine, and instantly I lost power.

Our race was over.

The team went to work on the engine but it was obvious there was going to be no chance of a miracle comeback, so instead we changed our focus on trying to get any points we could out of the race. They got the car to the point where I could get it back onto the track, but after two slow laps I headed into the pits again and waited. We'd done enough laps to be classified as a finisher, as long as we were out running when the chequered flag was waved.

So as Holden's David Reynolds was on his way to his first Bathurst victory, I chugged around for a couple of laps to ensure we were classified in 20th and last place, claiming 90 valuable championship points.

It proved to be extra important, given what had happened to McLaughlin with his Ford having engine failure halfway through the race, forcing him to retire. His Team Penske teammate Fabian Coulthard had now leapt over both of us in the championship after he finished third.

A post-mortem in the Triple Eight garage revealed it was a broken valve that had ruined our race. What was confusing for the mechanics was we'd put a new engine in the No. 88 car after Saturday's final practice session in a bid to improve my straight-line speed.

My home track on the Gold Coast was next and a conservative approach with fuel saw me finish second behind McLaughlin in the second race of the weekend, but it still meant that for the first time I had the lead in the championship.

New Zealand was next and Shane kept his local fans happy by winning the opening race at Pukekohe. I finished fourth, which was solid, but what wasn't solid was my stomach, as I was hit with a horrible bout of food poisoning on the Saturday night. It had knocked me for six and I was still in trouble the following morning. Nothing was staying down but I had to find a way.

As I walked to the start line for the second race our team physio Chris Brady had turned into my chief motivator. 'If there's any time in sport you have to dig deep, it's right now,' were his words.

They certainly resonated and I managed to find something when it mattered, holding off McLaughlin to win the race and, more importantly, take home the Jason Richards Memorial Trophy.

(Jason Richards had tragically lost his life to cancer in 2011 at the age of 35. We'd been teammates back in the Tasman Motorsport days and had run second at Bathurst in 2005.) Being the driver to collect the most points over the two races in Richards' homeland, I won the trophy, and it was an honour I cherished.

It also meant I went into the final round in Newcastle holding a 30-point lead. Given there were 300 points available over the weekend, 30 wasn't much, so there was absolutely no room for error.

Unfortunately, we made one.

In the opening race on the Saturday around the brand-new street circuit, McLaughlin had made a statement by qualifying in pole position while I'd done a reasonable job to start fifth on the grid. However, on turn two my world flashed in front of my eyes.

Nissan's Michael Caruso was in a tussle with Shane and had gone wide, and I saw an opening down on the inside. The problem was he corrected quicker than I'd expected and cut straight back across with his left rear tyre smashing into my right front wheel.

The impact was significant. My tyre exploded, sending me into the wall, which did a number on my steering. I couldn't believe I'd made such a stupid mistake. It was the wrong time and place to be doing that sort of move with the championship on the line.

The team managed to fix the problem with the car and I did rejoin the race later, but it was an ugly scenario given I was 13 laps behind McLaughlin.

My rival went on to claim victory in the 250km event, effectively snuffing out my title hopes. I'd struggled home in 21st, salvaging 42 points.

Dinner that night was like being in a morgue. My stupidity had been a kick in the guts to everyone, and there wasn't a lot of conversation going on around the table. McLaughlin now had a 78-point lead and he only needed to finish 11th or better the following day to win his maiden title.

After all the sacrifices I'd made that year to focus solely on winning this championship, I couldn't believe it had all been for nothing. There just seemed to be no justice in having done all this work only to blow it all with a terrible last round.

I knew I had to say something.

'This can't be happening,' I said. 'There is absolutely no way we can allow this to happen. I know it's a long shot, I know it most likely isn't going to happen, but can we please do ourselves proud and give it a shot tomorrow. Let's go out with pride, knowing we've given it everything.'

The mood seemed to change and when we reconvened in the lead-up to the final race, there was a different feel around the garage. If we were going to go down, it was going to be with a fight.

RD had spoken to Lowndesy, Shane and me and said everything was geared towards getting car No. 88 the most points. 'It's not over until it's over,' were the boss's parting words.

It was going to be a Triple Eight assault, and Shane started off by putting the pressure on McLaughlin from the beginning, with the two clearing out early.

Things started to get interesting when they pitted on lap 14, where McLaughlin was slapped with a drive-through penalty for speeding in pit lane as he tried to beat Shane out.

This sent him outside the top 20, but he quickly worked his way back towards the magical 11th position that he needed to deny us the title. However, a clumsy passing attempt that sent Simona de Silvestro into a spin saw the stewards hit McLaughlin with another penalty.

By this time I'd worked my way to second behind Shane, who then heeded RD's order and let me cruise by.

After the second safety car for the day went green with 22 laps remaining, McLaughlin had found his way back to 13th. Shortly afterwards he was involved in a three-car pile-up but the damage was only cosmetic.

While all this was happening, I was taking care of business.

McLaughlin had again recovered, and with three laps to go he passed Garry Rogers Motorsport's James Moffat to move into the critical 11th position. What he didn't realise was the Triple Eight ace up the sleeve, as Lowndesy had just put on new tyres and was on a mission to hunt down the entire field, which included McLaughlin.

By the start of the penultimate lap Lowndesy moved to 12th and was all over McLaughlin. Given the tight nature of the street circuit there weren't many passing opportunities, but Lowndesy isn't one of the greatest of all time for nothing.

On the uphill straight between turns one and two, Scott went wide and seemed to have pulled it off, then Lowndesy made his move. McLaughlin tried desperately to cover his line, but he was too late and as a result of the contact fired Lowndesy into the wall.

By this point I was oblivious to what was going on and had spent the last few laps looking up at the big screen, trying to see where McLaughlin's car No. 17 was positioned.

As I crossed the finish line to reach the chequered flag, I had no idea what it meant.

'Talk to me, guys. What's happened?' I said over the team radio.

I didn't get a response straight away, which made me more anxious, and then the radio came on air but all I could hear was screaming and yelling. Surely that could only mean one thing.

Finally my engineer Cauchi's voice broke through: 'We've won! We've won!'

My first thought was if this is a practical joke, it's a pretty bad one.

'We've won,' Cauchi repeated.

McLaughlin's penalty for his contact on Lowndesy had come through just as I'd crossed the line. The stewards had hit him with a 25-second penalty, which dropped him from 11th to 18th.

The 2017 Supercars Championship was mine.

All the sacrifices, all the pain, it had been worth it. And that's why my seventh title is my greatest achievement.

After the regulation burn-outs the presentation area wasn't ready, so I stopped at turn one and started the process of getting out of the car. By the time I did, Cauchi and my good mate and co-driver PD had jumped onto the track and were sprinting in my direction.

They both leapt into my arms and we were hugging in the middle of the track. It was a special moment and I already had plans to make this a memorable celebration.

First stop was the fountain out the front of Newcastle's famous Customs House. I jumped straight into it, which shocked the locals given it was often used by punters as a different kind of watering hole on their way home after a night out. I liked the idea that I'd started a tradition, and next year's winner was going to have to follow suit.

Then, after the champagne shower, when I got my hands on the trophy I'd been craving for 12 months, I made a detour on my way to the post-race press conference.

All week I'd been staring at the water in Newcastle Harbour thinking how nice it looked. Red Bull had a hospitality boat anchored there, so I charged up the ramp, grabbed a beer, necked it and then executed a perfect backflip off the deck and into the water.

The crowd on the boat erupted. It was a little loose and probably out-of-character, but this day was going to live in the memory bank for a long time and had to be celebrated accordingly.

No-one could believe we'd pulled it off. It just showed how bizarre motorsport could be.

I'd previously won championships with far superior equipment than the rest of the field, but that certainly wasn't the case this year. We'd just mentally hung tough and found a way.

It was funny because I knew how McLaughlin was feeling. I'd been that guy before – the one in the quickest car who'd done some amazing things throughout the season yet didn't come home with the trophy.

This time I did, and I wasn't taking my hands off it.

The following night I found myself standing in front of the entire Supercars fraternity getting interviewed at the annual Gala Awards, where I couldn't help but get emotional.

'Massive, massive sacrifices had to be made,' I said. 'It's pretty scary. I had to make some big calls at the end of last year. We've dug deep, made some sacrifices, kept the focus and got the job done.

'It was all or nothing. As I said, it's probably pretty sad, but this sport means everything to me and this trophy means everything to me.'

ROLAND DANE

Triple Eight Team Principal, Managing Director

'We were looking for a young driver to play a supporting role to Craig Lowndes, particularly with a view to partnerships for the enduro races at Sandown and Bathurst. Jamie was 22 and had equipped himself very well alongside Jason Richards in those two races in 2005, and that is really what put him very much on the radar. There were three of them on the radar – him, Mark Winterbottom and Will Davison – but Jamie was far and away the most enthusiastic, and he also had a very good track record with those two events that year. He wanted to get his bum in the car, to make sure he had a drive. And to be honest, that was all that mattered to him, and that was different from other people who were more concerned with earning money rather than looking at the long-term.

'He was exceptional out of the box for us, but we knew he was going to be better than we'd bargained for when he tested. He went out and won the Sunday race of the opening round in Adelaide, and it was very clear that by 2007 we had two drivers of equal stature in terms of ability to win races. Jamie started off, and the team started off that year, unfortunately in a very bad way with the suicide on New Year's Day of Jamie's number one mechanic. That shook the team as a whole, let alone Jamie. It took us longer that year to really find our feet, and it wasn't until we went to Winton in May that we won a race. We'd kicked off with Vodafone at the beginning of that year, and we were running competitively, but we just didn't manage to string it together until Winton. Broadly, that was because of the impact of losing our main character in the team make-up tragically at the beginning of the year.

'Then, by the back end of 2008, Jamie was extremely dominant. He had a very long run of race wins and obviously won a third Bathurst with Craig. Jamie was fundamentally the natural talent there, driving at a very, very high level, and then as the intensity of the game changed – and continues to change with other drivers getting more professional, along with the driving level overall and at the team operation level – the bar keeps rising, and Jamie has retained the ability to reinvent himself.

'As he got older he needed to reinvent the way he drove the car, because we switched from the older car to the project blueprint Supercar that ran until the end of 2012, then into the Car of the Future in 2013. Everyone had to adapt to the new car, new tyre size, the rear suspension layout, which was very different, and the way the car behaved. Jamie had to reinvent himself. I think the closest parallel for me in contemporary motorsport is the way that Valentino Rossi has reinvented himself. He has reached the end now, but certainly over 15 years of being very competitive in MotoGP he had to adapt his style to changing motorcycles and to meet the challenge of different competitors. Jamie has done a similar thing in Supercars.

'From a pure driving point of view, rather than an overall team point of view, his best performance was Adelaide in 2012 – the Saturday race, which was the first race after his father passed away. There were effectively two different strategies going on in the race because of safety cars – people were trying to stretch their fuel, others were saying, "No, I can't make fuel last. I'm going to go flat out and make an extra stop." Jamie and his engineer went for the later strategy, so he had to stop again, yet he took the lead on the last lap with a couple of corners to go to win that race, having done the extra pit stop over the people he was competing against.

'We have always prided ourselves on giving equal equipment to our drivers. If you try and treat them as equally as possible, then the only rule really in that situation is that they don't hit each other. Craig and Jamie did it in Tasmania in 2014, and I was furious with them afterwards. They were both at fault, to be honest; they were both dickheads that day. In 2016, Shane [van Gisbergen] and Jamie had an incident at Pukekohe – that one was more Jamie than Shane, compared to the one in Tasmania in 2014, which was six of one and half a dozen of the other and unnecessary.

'In 2017 he hadn't won for two years, and to be honest 2015 was the only year he didn't really turn up, and 2016 he was beaten by Shane. The only time I felt he really needed a kick up the arse was after 2015. I always said after running at the front as long as he had – winning six championships to that point – he was entitled to have a year where he wasn't quite as sharp. Going into 2016 with a new challenge and new teammate, Jamie rose to the occasion, and then in 2017 Penski was spending a fortune compared to us. It went down to the wire and they made mistakes over that last weekend – Scotty McLaughlin in particular. Jamie did what he had to do, winning the final race, and it was all he could do. He had to wait on the radio to find out whether he had won the championship or not. Scotty McLaughlin didn't handle the pressure that day, but he clearly went on to figure that out the following year, which was similar to what Jamie had done in 2007, to be honest.

'The only thing Jamie has really ever done wrong is not be Craig Lowndes. He came along when Craig was very much the man of the moment. Although he hadn't won the championship since 1999, Craig was still a dominant figure in the paddock. And there was Jamie stealing race wins and championships off him as Craig came second in the championship four times to Jamie. That probably hurt some of the fans – the dyed-in-the-wool Lowndesy fans. There was a great number of them then, and there still is. It's silly that Jamie's biggest crime was not being Craig Lowndes, but Jamie is also a pretty private person. He likes to have his privacy, which I think people, whether sports people or media people, are entitled to have. The people who do know him appreciate that he is very much his own person and is an extremely good communicator in the right circumstances, given the right platform. His filter is getting better, but certainly early on he was guilty only of telling the truth, sometimes when he would have been better advised to not tell all of it.

'He is very much a huge fan of the sport as well as a participant. He loves the sport, he loves the history of it, and he loves being a part of it. He said to me about three years ago that he'd like to think that he could do [a team management role] and wanted to prepare, to start thinking in terms of preparing himself and being a shareholder if I let him, and I said yes. He bought into the team with the aim of seeing where that took him over the next couple of years, and by the time we got to late last year he was ready to commit himself to taking over at the end of 2021.

'His passion for the sport is there, and he also wants to carry on being involved at a high level and creating the opportunity for himself. He didn't just want to be another person doing television or something. He wanted to do something different and potentially more meaningful.'

9
KATE

IT'S that unspoken bond where words don't need to be used. You are so in sync with one another that everything just feels right. Together you form an incredible team and these feelings are so rare; they're so strong that you'd be lucky to feel them once or twice in your life. It is true love, one that should be cherished and forever remembered. I had this with Kate . . . my Supercar.

It started with Betty, then there was Dani, Kate, Georgia, Elizabeth, Jen, Alana, Dassi, Bree, Meredith, Lindsay and Risa.

They're not the names of my ex-girlfriends: they're all my Supercars. And before you go jumping to any conclusions about the reasoning behind the names, I'm taking that to the grave.

It wasn't until I made it to Supercars that I started the practice, and you'd be surprised how much we actually talk to our cars when we're in the heat of battle. A bit of urging or sometimes cursing seems to have more impact when there's a name involved.

My favourite is clearly Kate, who has currently won more races than any other car in history.

She came into my life in 2010 when we first moved from Ford to Holden, but then the team built a new car that I moved into halfway through the season. However, something wasn't right and I went back to Kate for 2011 and 2012.

It was a relationship that flourished. Kate and I shared two of the most important moments of my career. She was with me in Adelaide, when I won the Clipsal 500 a week after my father passed, and then she got us over the line in Bathurst later that year with my good mate Paul Dumbrell.

Every time I spoke to any legends of the sport they'd say you must buy your old racecar when you retire. I wasn't quite sure about this practice – these cars aren't cheap and you literally need to take out a large loan – but the idea made a lot of sense when it came to Kate.

After the end of the 2012 season I approached RD and asked if I could purchase Kate. He gave me an amazing discount deal, and a meticulous restoration was soon underway.

This task was handed to one of my former mechanics, Garry Bailey, who had a shed up in Toowoomba. He had to strip the whole car back, and we waited 18 months for the original engine because it had been brand new when we'd won Bathurst, so it had to serve its time through 2013 and part of 2014.

All the original stickers were put back on. She had new tyres, brakes, rims – everything was exactly the same as when I raced her.

I'd always wanted to get my truck licence, and having to go pick Kate up inspired me to do it. Driving up and down the Toowoomba Range was an interesting experience for a rookie. I spent half the time on the phone to the Triple Eight crew who'd loaned me the transporter, trying to figure out how to get the engine brake to work for the run down the range.

At one stage in my life I'll build a house big enough to store all my former cars, but I decided Kate deserved to be put on display. I found her a home at the impressive Tailem Bend racetrack in South Australia.

I've also had one of my go-karts rebuilt, although I've struck trouble with getting my most successful Formula Ford from my mate Davo, who has it in his garage, given he also used it early in his career.

This need for speed is something that's hard to explain. If I'm not doing something that's on the edge and challenging, I get bored. Most things I do love in life are about going fast. Some of the best times of my life are when I'm on a dirt bike, or a mountain bike, tearing through the bush going seriously fast. Pushing the limits makes me happy, although I do have to rein myself in at times, considering I have a contract that says I need to be fit and healthy to drive a Supercar, which means no broken bones.

It's all about being calculated. I'll go and do a backflip off a rock into the water if I know it's deep enough, yet I might not go on the dodgem cars at the local show because the front wheel is rusted or there are old electrics, just on the off-chance someone could get electrocuted. Meanwhile, I will go skydiving because I know the probability of something going wrong is low, that if your first chute doesn't work for some crazy reason there is a second one available.

In a normal season there is a six-week break in the middle, so we have to find a way to replace the adrenalin rush that driving a Supercar gives us. The brain of a racecar driver needs to be challenged with speed and the risk factor it is used to, so during these times water skiing, kite surfing, motorbike riding or go-karting become important exercises.

There's a clear element of risk in this behaviour, and there have been plenty of concussions over the journey, but going fast makes me happy.

Unfortunately I feel like society is trying to slow everything down. Everything's becoming too sanitised, too boring. A perfect example of this was when I did a promotional shoot for Yamaha to showcase what their jetskis were all about.

We did some decent wave jumping and I was really getting some good air – the footage and photos were amazing. Yet the bean counters at head office shut it down because it was too dangerous, saying their products shouldn't be showcased like that. The official line was that the product should stay on the water. A couple of pen-pushers decided that. Please.

There is an asterisk with my need for speed and love of going fast – it's when I'm in the passenger seat.

Back in the early days, to earn pocket money, we did some driver training at racetracks, where people would come in and get the thrill of driving a Supercar or various high-speed vehicles. The car-makers often had events, and there was one particular Audi day at Calder Park, which was run by former touring car champion Brad Jones, that was memorable for all the wrong reasons.

I was working beside another driver, Christian Murchison, and we had to go out and set up the course in this flash RS6 Audi. We were putting out cones for a high-speed lane change where you'd drive at 120kph and then have to swerve to the next lane and keep the car under control.

We were told to keep the ESP – Electronic Stability Control – on at all times, but since we were professional drivers Murcho figured that wasn't required.

On a run-through he did a high-speed lane change where the car stepped out a bit. Murcho was trying to be funny and was playing it up as if he was out of control by yanking at the steering wheel. It was a bit of a laugh before suddenly it went a bit too far and we actually were out of control.

The car skidded up the road and ploughed into the wall head-on at 70kph. All the airbags went off and I got smacked in the face in the passenger seat, cutting my lip and giving me a bloody nose. Murcho had burns on his arm from the airbags and we had to quickly get out of the car because the airbags activating had filled the cabin with dust, which we found out later was toxic.

We brushed ourselves off and started to figure out what to tell Brad. He understandably wasn't happy, and with the clients about to arrive at the track on a bus we had to get rid of the car.

It wouldn't exactly be a good look for the customers if they saw the instructors smashing up the merchandise. We quickly got the wrecked car on a trailer, and then for the rest of the day we were basically telling people how to drive with a cut lip and bloody nose. My story to them was that I'd tripped over in the shower, and that's why I had two tampons stuck up my nostrils.

I hadn't learnt my lesson by this stage, with another special day at Sandown bringing me undone.

Will Davison and I were offering tips to people who would bring out their hotted-up cars and give them a spin around the Supercars track. It gave them the opportunity to really test their boundaries in a controlled environment, rather than doing it at an industrial estate, in the suburbs or on back roads down the bush.

Our job was to sit in the passenger seat and teach the drivers how to hit an apex, how to threshold brake and get the most out of their car. On this particular day one of the clients asked Davo if he could take the client's HSV Commodore for a lap. The owner wanted to know what time Davo could do in his car.

Davo wanted me to join him, and after initially declining, he twisted my arm and I got in.

'Mate, can you take it easy? All I've got is this shitty belt,' I said as I clipped in my basic road car seatbelt. He was wearing the proper full six-point racing harness.

Davo wasn't holding back as we zipped up the back straight, and I figured there was a bit of pride on the line as he wanted to show the guy how the professionals did it. When we got to the top of the hill and he backed off the throttle, the car surged.

Suddenly the steering went all heavy and Davo was pulling on it. I felt like I was pulling it with him because my mind was thinking what I would be doing, and he was doing exactly that.

Finally, the Commodore turned but it went too hard and started spinning out with my side crashing into the wall. It was ugly. Thankfully we'd survived the impact unscathed, but you couldn't say the same about the car.

Straight away Davo was stressing out because we'd just destroyed this guy's vehicle. There were pieces of it littered all over the track, including the front bumper bar.

'What am I going to say?' Davo kept asking me.

Technically, there was an issue with the car that had caused the accident, and that was the song I told him to sing: 'You've just got to tell the truth because at the end of the day it wasn't your fault.'

The owner of the car was understanding, although his wife not so much. Davo and I ended up doing a few free days for the driving school, who had to pay half the bill for rebuilding the battered Commodore.

It was actually good money back then – sometimes you'd do three or four sessions a week at $220 per day – but I finally pulled the plug after an incident at another high-performance day at Phillip Island in 2003.

This time I was in a Subaru, and the guy who was driving was doing a really good job, so I decided to give him more trust. I explained how he might want to apply the brake a bit later at the next turn. We were starting to push it a bit and he'd managed to work through a couple of slides, but then coming up to Lukey Heights, a famous section of the track that begins as a long left-hander, he started to panic out of nowhere.

The result was an out-of-control skid and we flew off into the gravel trap sideways, thankfully pulling up before the wall. I absolutely shat myself.

And I declared there and then I was finished with driver training.

I never went back.

However, I did break my golden rule one last time. We were at the Norwell Motorplex facility in Queensland doing a filming day, and my Supercar was running really rich with flames flowing out the back. While that was being looked at, this guy I knew, Robbie Bolger, had his Supercar there and urged me to hop in for a spin.

I'd been asked 50 times since the Phillip Island incident and had always said no, but for some reason on this day I jumped in the passenger seat.

We certainly had a crack down the back straight leading into a fast sweeper where things quickly went wrong. We speared straight off the track and were heading towards this huge sign that was supported by heavy duty H-beams.

If we hit the H-beam, anything could happen – the car could easily be cut in half. All of this was racing through my mind before I saw a ditch ahead of the sign. Luckily it was at a 45-degree angle to the way we were going, and somehow it kinked the car so that we just missed the H-beam.

To this day I'm not sure how it happened, but we somehow skidded down the grass and missed all the trees in the process. All I managed to say when we finally came to a rest was, 'Get me back to the pits.'

That was the last time I have ever been a passenger in a racecar.

How do I prepare for a date with Kate?

Race days are full-on, and that's even before you sit inside your Supercar.

Wake-up is usually between 6.30 and 7am, and then it's straight to the track, where all your meals for the day are served. A debrief with your engineers is the first port of call, where you talk about what happened the previous day, whether that be practice or qualifying, and then what the plan is for the race.

Data is looked over again – you forever have your head in the laptop – and then depending on what type of a race weekend it is, you may be required to go to the corporate box to shake some hands and chew the fat. There will be a signing session thrown in there with the fans, which can be taxing, so your focus through all of this period is to stay cool and conserve energy.

Then it's back to the truck for more hydration and food. And more strategy talk.

The key on race day is setting up the car for the conditions. My role is to work with the engineers, provide feedback and then nail down areas where the car can be improved.

If the data is telling us we are two-tenths of a second off the pace at a certain sector in qualifying, they'll come to me and ask why. Then together we'll workshop it; that two-tenths of a second becomes our entire focus.

There are many things it could be. The car might not be turning well into the corner. The data will show it's a medium-speed corner, so maybe if we increase the grip in the front it will find us the two-tenths.

When the car's out on the track all the basic information gets streamed straight to screens in a process called telemetry. Further information is gained when the car pits and a laptop is plugged into what's essentially a black box in the car, which then downloads all the data. There are over 100 different sensors on the Supercar, and they're triggering all the time, creating this massive data file. There are so many things that are being registered and reviewed.

The number of revs versus the rear-wheel speed will tell you something, then you can figure out how much wheel spin you have overall, so it will spit out different graphs on that. It can measure how far you're turning the steering wheel and what that does to the G-force.

There could be an issue with the front of the car where it's too high, so we're losing aerodynamics. The data engineers will spend all night looking at this, trying to figure out why the car won't turn at that particular corner.

Even when they come up with a solution of transferring grip from the rear to the front, it's my job to point out that I may need that rear grip for another corner in a different part of the track. Then we'll debate that and more than likely decide what corner is more important for lap time and commit to focusing on that.

Tyres take up a lot of our time.

Balancing fuel and tyres can win or lose you races. Generally, the more camber you run with on a tyre the more grip you get and the faster you go, but there's a risk of that tyre heating up on the inside edge and blowing up.

That gives you a 50–50 chance of finishing the race, but what those tyres have is pace, so you can be hard to catch. If you win, that's when you have to say hats off for being ballsy. But you're not going to get away with that all the time.

That's why our mentality has always been about being the best car overall and winning championships. We're not a team that flips a coin about whether you finish or not – we want to finish every race.

What the viewer at home on the couch watching a Supercars round doesn't realise is the amount of trickery that goes on between the teams. Every team listens to each other's radio frequency, so they know when their rivals are going to pit and what strategy they may be working on.

After a couple of years at Triple Eight we decided there was a need to run some deception and come up with codes to throw others off the scent.

Generally, it's all about the tyres. At some tracks it's faster to pit before your opposition, as the out lap on new tyres is faster than their in lap on old tyres – this is called an undercut. But on some tracks it's faster to pit after your opposition, as the out lap can be slower, due to the tyres not coming up to temperature quickly enough. In fuel races, the extra weight also slows you down.

These decisions vary at different tracks and in different races but, for example, if you're 10 laps into a race and you're starting to get to a point where you could pit, you want to do it before your opposition. If you call it over the radio, then the opposition will hear it and make sure they come in ahead of you. Pit stops can take around 25 seconds for fuel and tyres, barring a disaster.

So if you can get in and pit before your close rival, hopefully then you can undercut them on the out lap. Hence, why we needed codes for when the engineer tells the driver to pit or the driver wants to suggest it's time to do it. Although you have to keep changing those codes so that other teams don't work them out.

The first code we went with had to do with what name my engineer would call me. All the time it was 'J-Dub' but any time he used 'Jamie', that meant he wanted me to pit. So something that sounds innocent like 'Good job, Jamie' instead of 'J-Dub' meant to hit the pits.

On the steering wheel there's a 'Pit Confirm' button, so I would then push that to alert them I'd received the message.

The other good one is when the team might say, 'Box this lap' instead of 'Pit this lap', which you're hoping might throw your opposition out. They might react and pit early, which clears the track in front, and sometimes that's what you need depending on the circumstances of the race.

You have to be careful not to confuse yourself with all of these ducks and drakes. In the heat of the moment it's possible to forget the codes or get mixed up, since the codes are regularly changing. Putting my hand up here – there have been times when we've tried to be too smart and stuffed it up.

Often in the big races, where trickery isn't as important, you default back to basics so you don't make any mistakes. Generally, though, you have a clear plan and know what the secret calls are and use them whenever you can.

The pit-lane battles extend beyond the radio calls. There's a technique some teams use that makes it slightly harder to get into your pit box. Even though they're not pitting they can come out of their garage and pretend they're setting up, which means you have to drive around them when turning into your garage area.

There have also been examples of just one mechanic out sweeping his team's pit box at the exact moment you're turning in, which again means you have to travel further, and slower, to turn in. We're only talking about maybe half a second, but these are the little things that add up and can make a difference.

As a general rule, Triple Eight doesn't play these pit-lane games. We may have returned the favour to a rival from time to time, but generally it's a grey area we stay away from.

The beauty of a day in the life of a Supercar driver is that any or all of these things can impact you at any time.

It's funny but out of the whole week you feel the worst on race day. You train and live a healthy lifestyle so you feel a million bucks when you leave for the race meetings, but then by the time you get home on a Sunday night you're absolutely shot.

That's why I'm not a great celebrator after a successful race weekend – I literally have nothing left, mentally or physically.

Rather than sink a half a dozen beers or a bottle of red wine, I celebrate by getting into the pool in my backyard, where I just start swimming slowly. That's my secret ritual: an hour in the pool to keep the body moving while also clearing all the numbers out of my mind.

It's my brief nirvana before my mind inevitably starts thinking about my next date with Kate.

MARK DUTTON

Race Engineer 2007–2014

Triple Eight Team Manager

'I had been a race engineer for three years and was with Steven Ellery, the driver before Jamie. But when they signed up J-Dub, Ludo [Lacroix] was keen to be his race engineer, so I got demoted to a data engineer. It was actually my best performance review with Roland [Dane] and Ludo ever, because they were giving me less responsibility and a pay rise, which was still two-fifths of nothing. They said nice things to me as well, which was the one and only time.

'For 2006, Ludo was the race engineer and I was data engineer. Then the '07 season started and he wanted to go down a different path, so I got switched back to race engineer for J-Dub. And it was relentless from the start – you just wanted things to be right, and you did whatever it took to get it right. I remember having a bit of a laugh with the mechanics on the car the day that I was appointed. I cruised out and told them I was back as race engineer and said, "Welcome to Club 88. We work hard, we party hard." I told them that the first win we got we'd throw a big party, with kegs and the whole thing. I didn't think it was going to happen straight away, but in the first race in Adelaide he came third, and then he won the second race. We threw the party, which was cool, and J-Dub stumped up the cash to make it happen, so that was awesome.

'I didn't know that much about Jamie before he came. When I first heard he was going to be our new driver, I had this image in my mind of, I think it was from Tassie, where a throttle stuck or a brake pad failed or something happened, and all you saw was J-Dub spearing down the outside of everyone at a million miles an hour into the gravel trap. That image stuck in my head, and I'm like, *If that's a throttle stuck then why didn't he put the clutch in?* So I was thinking, *Hmmm, is this going to work?*

'I wasn't in the first interview he did with Ludo, but we had quite an open-plan layout, so I was listening in. I remember it was a good thing that he was asking so many questions. Some of them were quite obviously wrong – his opinions on the technical side of things – but he was still asking them. Ludo would have a bit of a chuckle, the way Ludo does, and then he would correct him. But the good thing was J-Dub didn't stop. He's not expected – none of the drivers *should* be expected – to understand the technicalities the same way as the engineers, because otherwise we would have no use for the engineers. But he just wanted to know. He wasn't afraid, which I really, really liked. Some of the questions were very intuitive and smart, and some not as much, but it didn't matter – the only dumb question is the one you don't ask. I really liked that from the get-go, to hear him, wanting to improve, wanting to absorb as much information as he could. I thought that was a really good start.

'We came super close to winning it in the first year. Working together, you get to understand what the other person is saying, things like that. I was quite repetitive in my questioning when we set up the car in a practice session. I would ask him the same questions, and he was very good at answering. We were also very good together in the sense that he was doing his job, and I was doing my job, but we both helped each other do each other's job. The main thing was he wasn't trying to engineer a car – he was just trying to give the best information he could. It was good, honest information, without trying to say too much.

'The other good thing with Jamie is I still think, as a test driver, he has the best feel of any of drivers I've seen or worked with. Just the consistency and not over-driving the car. Back then the tyres in practice were so rubbish compared to these days, so to extrapolate the data you had to say, 'Okay, *this* is what we got with *this* level of tyre; we think the next step requires *this* once we've got good rubber.' We got quite good, and the chemistry was showing up at qualifying in particular. That's when you'd have to make the biggest step up and figure out what this rubbish rubber was doing, and what good rubber is going to do, because his feedback was so good. Once you get that momentum and they are still in qualifying, when they start knowing and trusting what is underneath them, being able to know what is going to happen next, when the car feels like this, or if I put this input I know what the output will be before it happens – they become very hard to beat.

'Definitely the stand-out drive has to be the emotional one after his father passed, particularly because we hadn't qualified well. We just went for the "hero or zero" strategy – we were just going to do quali laps for the whole race. I said, "We are going to juice you up, you don't have to conserve, you just have to go flat out and show us what you've got. Don't show us how well you can conserve fuel, just show us your speed, mate – you're a true racer." That was an amazing race, and it was really, really special to be a part of it. Everyone had the option to try and be super conservative on the fuel and do one less stop. The other option, the one we went for, was to do the extra stop, get the fuel and you go flat out to make up that extra time in pit lane. We went for it and the best thing was that it was all on him, just going as fast as he could, true racer stuff. It was awesome.

'There were lots of cool moments along the way. The times he put it on pole, and it sounds like a back-handed compliment when he says, 'Mate, the car was so hooked up you could have put it on pole.' It is one of those things, as a race engineer who has worked with Jamie to give him a car like that, and he's singing the praises that highly . . . that's pretty special. There have been lots of little things that people don't always see behind the scenes, where we are doing enduros and he's in the lead, gapping the field, conserving fuel and conserving tyres. He's doing all four at once so well, and you're going, "Gee we are working well here." That is next level.

'J-Dub had this single-mindedness; he wanted to be the best at Supercars. He didn't go and race other things in other categories during that time, which some people like Shane [van Gisbergen], who loves it when he is just racing everything. That works well for Shane. I think Jamie brought a new level to the series and the sport in Australia, for professionalism and just being an athlete. Jamie wasn't athletic, so to speak, to begin with, but he was an athlete in his professionalism – he wanted to get that right, to put all his eggs in that basket, to focus on that and demand that the people around him put that effort in. He wasn't afraid to question people if they weren't, and as you go along you work out the right way to ask questions and the right times to review things.

'The good thing is Jamie's mentality, which he got from his dad – they were very good at doing things right the whole time. When he was karting he would tell stories about how they were the only ones in the paddock who had the full set of spare nuts and bolts, and everyone would come to them, since they were always the organised ones. That has worked very well with the Triple Eight mentality, which has obviously come from Roland. So you have all those things coming together – that desire to keep wanting to win, to keep being better and not being complacent, not partying too hard . . . For me, that would be the hardest thing if I was in his shoes – I would have been ripping it up a bit more – but, no, he kept the focus.

'He was always focused on the next one and working hard. When we'd have a purple patch with him and a good run, you never took it for granted. We were never like, *We've got the next one nailed*. I can honestly say I never once thought that. You always did your preparation, and we got some amazing opportunities back then, like racing overseas. We had quite a good record of turning up to a new track and winning. When you're going to a new track it is such a good leveller – we're all rolling in with the same amount of info and practice on this track. So then it's like, Who can nail it? Who can do it the best? The feeling you would have when you got that right was huge; it was such a good motivator.

'I tell this story to the engineers about tyre pressures. We were at the Circuit of Americas [in Austin, Texas] for the first time, and through all the practice sessions we were P17 [17th position], and we were like, Has everyone stepped up? Or have we dropped the ball or something? What have we missed? We just stuck to our program, stuck to our guns, and we ended up doing a tyre-pressure change and went from P17 to P1. We got four pole positions, won three races and P2 in another race. It was obviously an amazing feeling to get it right, but it is an important story to tell the engineers about attention to detail.

'It is really interesting with J-Dub – he is one of the best public speakers I've seen; he is so funny. When he talks to a group, he engages so well and he's got such personality. In the early days he was more determined and focused on doing his procedure. If his prep work is an ice bath and then leave five minutes to get to the car, he doesn't want to break that, so that may mean he walks past fans or is in a bit of a hurry. He was trying to be that pure athlete, and the level of professionalism and consistency he was aiming for meant that he had to make a few sacrifices. And that was with us too.

'Sometimes, we would have to push him hard to be on time for debriefs, because his getting-out-of-the-car procedure would take nine-and-a-half minutes, and we had a debrief eight minutes after it or something like that. Roland would be shouting, "Where's Jamie?!" and stuff, but you had to change the schedule because he has his process and his procedure. He's feels like if he doesn't do it then he won't be able to give his hundred per cent, so you could see there is no way he's not giving a hundred per cent. He was like, "Sorry, this is what I need to do to give a hundred per cent, so this is what I am going to do time in and time out".

'You can throw in a bit of tall poppy syndrome in there as well, which is a bit of the Australian way. Particularly when your teammate is Lowndesy, the ever-bubbly one. He could get out of the car, even if it had just burnt to the ground, still smiling. Whereas with Jamie if the car had burnt to the ground he'd be devastated. It's only because his teammate is laughing and smiling that it exaggerates some of the responses to Jamie. Sometimes Jamie's response was the natural one.

'For me, there is no need for Jamie to retire right now – I think he could keep driving up at the top, getting pole positions, winning races and possibly championships into the future. He's made his decision, but I can say with an unbiased opinion that I still think he has got the goods.'

10

THE SIMPLE LIFE

THERE is a clear distinction between the simple life and the easy life. Don't be confused into thinking they're the same thing.

When you're working your arse off day in day out, don't ever be worried about missing out on the easy life. The easy life will always be there, waiting, ready to wash you away.

But the simple life is all about trying to declutter the things you don't need to be doing. There is so much going on nowadays that you need to stop doing the things you don't want to do. And by extension, stop dealing with people you don't want to deal with.

I've started asking myself in various situations whether what I'm doing is wasting time or not. Should I be spending all this time arguing with somebody or putting in the effort to make somebody happy when it may not be relevant to my life down the track?

We are all guilty of spending time on things that we shouldn't. A lot of people would say, well, that's everyday at work then. I can see where they're coming from. The way we live now, we're all wrapped up in the economy, programmed to work five to six days a week, do these long hours, earn money and then go and buy stuff that half the time doesn't make us happier.

Sometimes it feels like we're all in a big rat race, trying to keep this enormous economy wheel turning. Maybe the Native Americans and First Nations peoples had it right: they'd focus on hunting for food and supplies, then spend the rest of the time building their community and doing whatever they wanted to do.

The hippie life also massively appeals to me. Why not just stop? Go bush and hunt, live in a world that doesn't revolve around money?

It has merit, but at the same time I get massive satisfaction out of achieving things, setting goals and reaching them. These goals can be as simple as mowing the lawn. I'm at my happiest and most relaxed when the front lawn is absolutely mint. I get huge satisfaction out of those things, so that's why I keep doing them. I try to look for perfection, because that pursuit has always given me a great feeling of contentment.

For some people, working hard, getting satisfaction out of that hard work and a sense of achieving something is how they are wired. For others, it could be sitting on the beach and watching the sun go up one side and down the other.

There is no right or wrong answer, but what you should avoid is being trapped in something that you look back on and say, *That was a boring part of my life and I feel like I've wasted all this time.*

Part of the simple life is embracing the 'less is best' philosophy. Going for a walk on the beach is the simplest of things to do, but there's nothing I enjoy more. We always wonder: is having more better? It's definitely not.

A perfect example is when I take my ski boat out on the water now. Back in the day you'd put your waterskis on and then off you'd go. Now it's so much more complex – you not only take your skis but also your kneeboards, tubes, wakeboards, wakesurf boards. On and on and on it goes.

So now you ask yourself: Am I having more fun in the boat with 15 different activities than when I just had the waterskis? The answer is no.

This is one practical example of how we have the tendency to over-complicate things. I'm now chasing a life where I'm trying to continue working hard but minimising the clutter.

And I didn't have to look too far for inspiration on this front, with my long-time co-driver leading the way.

I couldn't help but smile as Paul Dumbrell pulled up outside the hotel.

I'd just arrived in Melbourne to prepare for the Sandown 500, and here was my mate sliding into the car park in a little Volkswagen Polo that must have been close to 20 years old.

PD could buy any car he wanted, yet here he was happily driving around in his wife's VW Polo. They'd just started a family, which required a bigger safer vehicle, so he'd purchased a brand-new Porsche for Rosie to get around in and he'd taken over her set of wheels. But rather than trade it up for a fancier option, he was loving zipping around in the old car. It was getting him from A to B, it was cheap to run, and you didn't have to give it a second thought.

I'm sure there were some raised eyebrows when we drove into Sandown in the VW Polo, which was probably worth around $3000, to get ready to hop into our $600,000 Holden Commodore.

My title defence in 2018 had started with a very simple negotiation with RD over my contract status.

'I'd like to continue driving in 2019,' I told him.

His reply was simple: 'Sure, no problem.'

We did have a wider conversation on how the future looked for me as I'd been thinking a lot about the bigger picture. I loved the sport and wanted to remain a key part of it. One option we discussed was buying into Triple Eight and becoming a stakeholder in the business.

RD was open to that and a potential move into team management was also put on the table. He was keen to reduce his responsibilities over the next few years, and when I stopped driving – neither of us were sure when that would be – the logical move would be to potentially slide into his seat.

That was still some way off in the future, but the seed had been planted.

*

As was predictable after his 2017 final-race disappointment, Scott McLaughlin came out firing in the new season and seemingly lived on the podium. My teammate Shane van Gisbergen was doing a good job chasing while we weren't too far away in third place.

My love affair with the Townsville Street Circuit had again helped me in the championship, with another victory there making it ten wins from 20 starts in Far North Queensland. And I'd also won the race leading into Sandown at a new event, the Bend SuperSprint, which was at the impressive Bend Motorsport Park in South Australia.

Sandown had always been a happy hunting ground for PD and me, and he seamlessly made the transition from the VW to the eight-cylinder Commodore by getting us a great start. He found the lead on turn one and from there we were basically never headed.

It was one of those rare afternoons where everything worked like clockwork. It was a banner day for Triple Eight. For the first time in the race's history one team filled the top three positions, with Shane coming home second and Lowndesy third.

The team couldn't be better placed as we went into Bathurst, where my run of outs had now stretched to five editions of the Great Race.

That wasn't *technically* true, given I'd tasted victory at Mount Panorama in 2017 in the Bathurst 12-hour event. It was my first venture into the world of GT racing, or sportscar racing, and it was a lot of fun driving a Ferrari for a change – although it was a crazy ride.

The event was part of the Intercontinental GT Challenge, which involves three races, another 12-hour and a 24-hour race, at different venues around the world. Australian drivers ride together with teams from Europe, who obviously race GT cars all year, and it was an interesting mix.

First we had to get used to driving on the other side of the car, given they were European models. This wasn't easy, as racing is all about the flow, having the Supercar just centimetres away from the wall and getting that rhythm.

You get really good in a right-hand-drive Supercar at knowing where the corners are and almost being able to put your hand out the window and touch the walls. So you can imagine how much your mind gets thrown out when you're sitting over on the opposite side of the car.

This happened to me all the time in the GT, particularly going over Skyline, the right-hand kink over the top of the hill at Bathurst. I was constantly finding myself feeling out of whack because I always felt wide, and your natural instinct from being in a Supercar is that if you're in that position you're going to crash.

Muscle memory is a weird thing and it takes a lot to change it. I was missing apexes all over the place, for one. Another difficult part is that the driving position in the Mercedes GT car is a lot further back than the Supercar – you almost feel like you're sitting on the back wheels.

Lowndesy and I teamed with Finnish driver Toni Vilander in a Ferrari 488, and I actually got us the win by chasing down my regular teammate Shane with 40 minutes remaining. It was a good mix because the European drivers were clearly more skilled in the cars, but the local knowledge around Bathurst meant the Aussies more than pulled their weight.

Previously I'd stayed away from doing too many other events outside of Supercars for two reasons. First, I was very much a homebody, and second, I found that committing myself totally to an entire Supercars season of 14 rounds was enough of a mental and physical challenge.

The only overseas race I'd taken part in was the Race of Champions, in which drivers from all over the world who'd been crowned the best in their country's respective series come together and compete.

There are four types of vehicles involved, and you change over to a different one for each race. For example, the first race you might be in a Super Truck, and then for the next race you'll be driving an Audi R8.

The format is interesting too. It takes place in a stadium that has an inside track and an outside track. You do two laps and then cross over and do two laps on the other circuit, with the winner being the driver who clocks the fastest time. And it's a knockout competition, so you have to win to survive. My first year was in 2012 in Thailand, and I was all at sea as I struggled to come to grips with the left-hand-drive machinery.

Two years later I travelled to Barbados, where I made the semifinals, eventually being eliminated by Formula 1 star David Coulthard, who went on to win. He's a great guy – one of the funniest bastards I have ever met. He would be one of the last to leave the bar each night, and then he would go and drive out of his skin the next day.

Earlier I'd provided one of the biggest shocks of the competition by knocking out reigning champion Romain Grosjean in a Super Truck, and then taking out NASCAR star Kurt Busch in an Audi R8 in the quarterfinal stage.

The semifinal was again in the Audi R8, and I went down by a mere 17 hundredths of a second.

There had been plenty more opportunities to travel and compete around the world, but it wasn't something I enjoyed. There's a simple reason: I get homesick.

I first discovered this when I was ten years old and went away to a Scout camp. I got gripped by fear on the second day and escaped the camp to ring Dad in tears, begging him to come and get me.

The same thing happened to me when I was in my early 30s on a trip to Las Vegas with a group of mates who I'd grown up with. It was an end-of-season boys' trip, and we were supposed to be there five days. After having a massive first night I woke up the next morning and just had to get home. I rang my personal assistant telling her to find a ticket. She initially said there were no flights other than one for $5000, and I told her I'd pay $50,000 just to get me home.

It was weird because I was with my mates and Las Vegas is such an awesome place, but sometimes I'm overcome by this need to be at home. I don't know what it is but it just comes over me, so since then I have been wary about being away for too long to avoid that homesickness.

Bathurst was almost like a second home, given how many times I'd been to the mountain, and I knew there was only one way to approach my 2018 visit. Surely, anything that could go wrong had already gone wrong. There couldn't be anything left. Every bit of bad luck in the Bathurst 1000 had struck us, so we tried to flip the narrative to being ultra-positive.

Once again we had a fast car, which we'd shown throughout qualifying, and after Saturday's Top 10 shootout we'd clinched second place on the starting grid, alongside Dave Reynolds's Erebus Motorsport Commodore.

There was certainly no decluttering possible at Bathurst. It was a beast in more ways than one and, being the biggest event on the Supercars calendar, the distractions are multiplied at the Great Race, with corporate garage tours, photos and TV interviews all coming at you, which is why Triple Eight has a one-hour lockout rule. That's our own time to prepare, and generally I'll hop onto the massage table for a tweak to get the body loosened up. Then with 20 minutes to go before we have to be on the grid, I'll make the dash from the truck to the garage.

More discussion with the engineers will take place then, to see if there have been any changes to the plans or the weather strategy. I have to be in the car five minutes before the start of the session to make sure everything is working – the radio, the air ventilation, everything. Then I'll leave pit lane and get the car around to the grid, where it sits for 30 minutes before the race starts. This is basically so fans and VIPs, who have paid a hefty premium, get the chance to wander around and see the cars close-up.

On a hot day this is far from ideal preparation, so I try to sneak back to the garage to keep cool before going back to the car with five minutes on the clock until the warm-up lap. A practice start is crucial here, and you try and get the temperature up quickly on the tyres during the lap.

It's funny how much focus is on the start of a race like Bathurst, given it goes for six-and-a-half hours, but the pressure is intense. Any mistakes can come back to haunt you.

A Supercar is not easy to get moving quickly – it's hard work getting this big 1300kg mass to do what you want. All the car wants to do is spin the rear wheels, the mass of the car wants to stay still, and the engine wants to drive the car forward via the rear wheels. Physics aren't on your side.

The key is to find the balance – not too much wheel spin and not too much clutch spin, since the car can go from zero to 100kph in first gear. We rate our starts by how long it takes to get from zero to 100kph. A good start (in dry conditions) is three-and-a-half seconds, a bad start is over four seconds.

So what is the best balance? The handbrake in a Supercar is electronic – it's a button on the steering wheel. You then dip the clutch and work the throttle, which controls the flow of power from the engine to the wheels.

With a Supercar, if you give it five-per-cent throttle the engine is on the 7500 rev limiter. On the other hand, holding onto it and trying not to stall is also a big challenge. The key is to get the throttle up to approximately 50 per cent as you hold the handbrake on and clutch in, waiting for the red light to go on the starting board. Once on, it will go off anywhere between three and five seconds later to signal the start of the race.

This guessing game about the red light keeps you on your toes. Once it does go out, you have to drop the handbrake, then drop the clutch and throttle all the way down to launch.

Touch wood, I have never stalled on the grid, but I've been bogged down a few times, which means I've been caught being really low in the revs and unable to move very far. The worst result is if you get the wheels spinning. That means you're not going anywhere, while others will be quickly sailing past.

The importance of the start varies from track to track. With tight-turning circuits like Homebush in Sydney, for example, it's difficult to pass around there. Nailing the start can often ensure victory.

There are many advantages for leading a race, but clear airflow is the biggest. It means the car runs cooler – you have more power as a consequence and the tyres don't heat up as much.

The thought of getting out in front early and avoiding trouble sounded like the perfect plan, but unfortunately I was tardy off the start this time, which allowed Reynolds to skip clear and his teammate Anton de Pasquale to come across from position three in front of me.

Shane also had a better start than I did and was also ahead, so the race was barely 30 seconds old and I'd gone from second to fourth.

When the race found its rhythm after the first pit stop, PD got us up to second place at the 40-lap mark. Everything was looking good until his voice came across the team radio, alerting us that something felt odd with the brake pedal.

That didn't sound right, and just as we started to compute this information things got decidedly worse. Smoke started to appear from the front of the car. Then suddenly the right-front wheel detached itself from the Commodore going into turn one.

I couldn't believe it. I stared at the television screen in total disbelief. How could this be happening to us? Losing a wheel was a new item to add to our Bathurst hoodoo list.

As he'd just gone past the pits, PD had to limp the full 6.213km back around the track at slow speed. The initial diagnosis was that a wheel nut wasn't quite fully tightened at the car's previous stop. The crew managed to repair the worst of the damage – a new front splitter, which had been ground away, and a new wheel safety clip – and sent PD back into the race, albeit two laps down.

It was so deflating, and while we progressively repaired the car further at subsequent stops, we were never able to make up the lost time. We did manage to get back onto the lead lap but it was a bridge too far, and we finished in tenth place.

The team's anger and disbelief was tempered by the fact that Lowndesy had managed to win his seventh Bathurst crown, with Steven Richards.

It was all the sweeter given my teammate had announced that this was going to be his final year as a full-time driver. At the age of 44, he was hanging up the helmet – although he still planned to dust it off for the endurance events.

The shock of the lost wheel lingered for a few days. I couldn't help but wonder what could possibly happen next.

I did know one thing . . . I just wanted to go for a walk on the beach.

11

THOSE WERE THE DAYS

IT'S the one saying that tips me off, and without fail I cringe every time I hear it: 'Those were the days.'

There's no doubt the days that came before us were good – go back 20 years in motor racing and those were good days.

But we're living in the *now*. These are *our* days, and it's no good reminiscing on 20 years ago all the time. Let's just worry about these days and make these ones better, maximise what we've got right now.

Instead of always looking back, we should learn what made those things great 20 years ago and then adapt them to the present.

I'm forever grateful that sport has taught me the ability to move on and put things in perspective. To enjoy the amazing era we live in, where the world is such a wonderful place, and not spend life worrying about something that didn't happen or might not happen.

This mantra was about to be put to the test – change on a number of fronts was set to send my life in a new direction.

There was a dogfight going on.

Triple Eight weren't used to being in this position and we didn't like it. Scotty McLaughlin had won the championship in 2018 and the dominance of his Team Penske Ford Mustang had gone to another level in the first half of the 2019 season.

Race wins were becoming harder and harder to come by because of what McLaughlin was doing. I'd gone through the opening five months of the season without a victory before finally getting my hands on the champagne up on the top step in Ipswich, Queensland.

That's why tensions were high when we arrived in New Zealand for the Auckland SuperSprint. There were only five events remaining, and Triple Eight desperately needed to fight its way back into the championship race.

We'd done a good job in the opening 70-lap race on Saturday, with Shane and me crossing the finish line in first and second, only for the stewards to intervene.

They decided to impose a 15-second penalty on me for a second-lap collision with Nick Percat, which meant I dropped down to sixth.

I was disappointed by the decision. I felt I'd been bottled up in the corner and Percat had come down harder than I'd expected. Could I have done more to avoid the situation? That was the question, and my view was clearly different to the stewards.

McLaughlin had struggled home in fifth before getting bumped up a spot after my penalty.

That whole scenario stoked my fire even more for the Sunday race, and we were in a good place early until 13 laps in when chaos hit with the introduction of the safety car.

Normally the safety car emerges from the pits in front of the leader, controlling the pace of the field until the hazard has been cleared. The problem was the hazard, which in this case was Dave Reynolds's Commodore, had already managed to limp back to the pits under its own steam, but the safety car was already out on the circuit.

This was where things became messy.

I'd been leading the race but pitted once the safety car had been called while a few other cars stayed out, which meant they were now in the lead. The issue was that the officials still thought I was in front when I emerged from pit lane. So when I came across the safety car I was confused to see orange flashing lights, which was the signal to stay behind it. The green lights should've been flashing until they caught up with the leader of the race.

In the lead-up to the race my engineer David Cauchi had reminded me not to get caught behind the safety car – it was a circuit where there had been confusion in the past. As I slowed for the safety car he was screaming in my ear, 'You are not the leader. You are not the leader. Do not get caught behind the safety car!'

I waited and waited for what seemed like forever but was probably only ten seconds. The officials had clearly made a mistake; they just hadn't worked out who the leader was.

Really, it was a case of damned if you do, damned if you don't. If I stayed behind the safety car because they had made a mistake, I'd be guaranteed to run last. If I passed the safety car, there would be a 50–50 chance they'd put their hand up and admit the error.

I took the second option. I figured the only way to get the right sequence for the safety car and to protect the integrity of the race was to go past it.

Then all hell broke loose because the cars behind me didn't follow my lead. It was a shambles and there were all sorts of mixed messages happening in pit lane, with several cars severely disadvantaged by it. For others, it gave them a huge leg-up.

I basically had one of my legs cut off, so to speak, with the stewards hitting me with a pit lane drive-through penalty, which blew up my race. I was an angry man when I got to the finish line in 16th place as McLaughlin claimed a record-breaking 17th win of the season.

When a television camera was placed in front of me, that filter I'd worked on in recent years disappeared. It was the old straight-shooting J-Dub who gave his thoughts on the safety car debacle.

'They should have had green lights on. I'm sure somewhere in the rule book they're allowed to keep the yellow lights because that's for a car in the wall in a dangerous position. But that wasn't the case today. They should have had green lights on; I wasn't the leader of the race.

'The problem is you've got all the drivers, you've got everyone here, this is our life, you know? And we're pushing bloody hard.

'And you've got people making decisions that are just cruising back, having a few glasses of red [wine] each night, and rocking up to the track and the brain's not with it. They're not operating at the same level as the teams are operating at.'

My explanation wasn't well received by the powers that be, and while I realised soon after that I may have gone too far, I was disappointed my chances in the race had been taken away from me. I knew I'd technically broken a rule, but I needed to win that race – it was bloody important to us and we'd given everything to get in a position to pull it off, only for an error by someone else to take that away.

When the dust settled I released a statement, explaining how when I'd asked myself if the comments about the stewards were necessary, the answer was no.

Did they help to fix the situation? No. Was I being a good role model by having a crack at the stewards? No.

Looking back, I regret the red wine comment and put it down as one of those experiences where you live and learn. To the stewards' credit they gave me the opportunity to learn, at the next race weekend, in Bathurst.

I was invited to the race control-room, and it was a real eye-opener to see how much actually goes on during a race meeting. The stewards aren't just dealing with the race – they're dealing with what's happening in pit lane and with all the staff around the circuit.

When I was in there, they had an incident with a flag marshal who'd become unwell during the race, and they were trying to work out whether they needed to throw the safety car out in order to get this marshal back to the pits for medical attention.

I was blown away with how much stuff they had going on that was outside the racing competition. It was a good experience for me to understand the difficulties that certainly made me further regret my comments in New Zealand.

However, we did manage to find a positive in the whole episode. I was able to work behind the scenes with the software team and help improve the systems they were using to track the lead car during races.

I know it sounds obvious about tracking the leader of the race, but when there are cars going everywhere into the pits it can be really difficult to determine the leader, which is why they rely heavily on the software. I made some suggestions about upgrading it to ensure we didn't have a repeat of what'd happened in Auckland.

It was almost a welcome distraction for my return to Bathurst. There was a freshness about this year's campaign, even though we were winding back the clock.

After seven years together PD had decided to hang up his helmet, and so I was reuniting with Lowndesy, which was now allowed in the rules because he'd retired from full-time driving.

Surely it was the curse-breaker: teaming up with the man who had won the great race the most times and was the defending champion.

While everyone was pumping up Lowndesy as being my good-luck charm – we'd driven together at Bathurst four times and won three of them – I always say you make your own luck.

What I was most proud of was the fact that every year our Triple Eight car contributed to the drama of the race. Whether that be winning or running out of petrol, we always seemed to be in the mix, and I'd much rather be talked about than running mid-pack and not even be noticed.

There was plenty to talk about in the 2019 Bathurst 1000, with conversations going on for days afterwards. Once again it was a bizarre edition of the Great Race where at various stages we looked like the winner, particularly at the halfway mark when Lowndesy had us in the lead.

Sometimes, as a team, you roll the dice on a tactic. At the 30-laps-to-go mark, often a call is made because you know you're not going to make it on fuel unless a safety car is called out. You only use half the fuel on a safety car lap compared to a normal green lap, which means you can take a punt and not pit, hoping a safety car near the end of the race enables you to get to the finish line with enough fuel.

On this occasion we decided with ten laps remaining to come in for a splash-and-dash, which means you don't fill up with fuel – you only give it a splash – but remain on the old tyres. In hindsight, that was our mistake. We decided not to change the tyres, as that would've taken another five seconds in the pits, resulting in us slipping down a couple more positions.

I emerged from the quick stop in fourth position, and we thought the first three cars were going to be tight on fuel, which would give us a chance. But the old tyres came back to haunt us; it made it far more difficult to pass other cars and, despite throwing everything at him, I failed to get past James Courtney. He claimed the last spot on the podium.

It was a missed opportunity for us. New tyres with fuel in that last stint could've resulted in a whole different story, but McLaughlin had won again, although there was a lot of controversy around the victory.

His team, DJR Team Penske, had ordered their sister car driven by Fabian Coulthard to slow down under the safety car late in the race. This tactic of bunching the field up and holding them back allowed McLaughlin to pit for extra fuel and come out still leading.

Lowndesy was furious, saying it wasn't in the spirit of the race to manufacture the result. While I wasn't against teamwork, it did seem to be a step too far and the stewards certainly thought it was a few steps in the wrong direction.

For a week the result was still provisional before the stewards finally allowed McLaughlin to keep the race, but they dumped Coulthard from 6th to 21st and fined Team Penske $250,000 – the largest fine in Supercars history. They also deducted 300 points from their team's championship tally. Later, they were given a penalty for breaching engine regulations at Bathurst, which further infuriated all the other teams.

It was the beginning of the end for Team Penske. Everything that went on at Bathurst, and the significant fallout, made the US-based owners realise that they couldn't be as adventurous with things in Australia like they did back at home.

Pushing the envelope is almost accepted in the US. They thrive on testing the limits from a technical point of view, trying to find any advantage. And if you do get caught it's almost met with, 'Oh yeah, you got me. Ha ha,' and then everyone moves on quickly. That's not the case in Australia. You can get caught jaywalking and end up on the front page of the paper with the whole community outraged over your actions. As a society, we don't like people bending the rules, and when you get caught it is massively frowned upon.

That was the sort of backlash Penske copped. Rather than sweep it under the carpet, Supercars made a statement by coming down hard. (Penske only lasted one more year and left Supercars at the end of 2020.)

We did manage to salvage something by taking out the 2019 Endurance Cup, for the best-performed pairing over the three endurance events. Lowndesy and I had won one event at the Sandown 500 and one event on the Gold Coast to win the trophy, while McLaughlin wrapped up the championship.

Another third place in the drivers' title left me pondering many things, including a question that was becoming more relevant and pressing by the day.

'Am I enjoying this?' I'd started to ask myself, and I knew that wasn't a good thing. I was getting to the end of the week and questioning whether I was moving forward.

I was busier than ever before, given I'd just joined the Supercars Commission and was expanding my business interests with a carwash venture on the Gold Coast and Brisbane. What concerned me was there was a sense that I was just ticking boxes rather than enjoying life.

This was all outside of the racing – I still loved driving a racecar as hard and as fast as I could. My mentality in that respect has never changed, but I needed better balance.

That was easier said than done.

The Supercars Commission was very much a passion project. I'd hooked my wagon to the future of the sport, so getting on the rule-making body was an important step. There were obviously politics involved in the process – there are only four team representatives and I wrote a letter to all the other team owners, declaring that I wasn't a puppet for RD.

My motivation was to help motor racing grow and make sure it was still one of the best sports in the country for the next 20 years. While I respected RD's opinion, I had my own views, and that's what I would be bringing to the table.

Working hard wasn't an issue for me, since it had been drilled into me from a young age, but I was becoming more and more aware of the need to do things differently. I was approaching a new phase in my life. I'd realised this had to be all about quality not quantity. Instead of doing four things on the weekend, I just needed to do one thing really well, and if that's going up the mountain to watch the water flow down the river, then so be it.

Life balance was becoming something to work towards.

For so much of my life I've just focused on one thing. I'd completely surrounded my life with driving. I'd obviously enjoyed all the trophies, seeing my name being a part of history and our team breaking records, but in many ways it had got me out of whack.

At different stages it was me who chose to lock down and put the blinkers on, but overall I hadn't been able to find the right mix.

I wanted to change that.

Spending your whole life working and not playing is clearly not good. Going out and having a few social drinks now and then is fine – actually, it's probably a good thing. Having some bad takeaway food once in a while to break up all that healthy eating is okay, too.

You don't have to balance *every* meal, you don't have to balance *every* day, and you don't have to balance *every* month. You just have to balance your *life*.

This new attitude didn't mean I was ready to pull the pin on driving, and once again another very quick conversation with RD resulted in a contract extension. I'd just turned 37 but I wasn't ready to retire, so we agreed to push everything out another year.

It wasn't the only question people were asking in the lead-up to the 2020 season-opener in Adelaide, given the bombshell Holden had dropped. The iconic Australian brand was being retired. The move followed the end of local production in 2017 and confirmation a couple of months earlier that the Commodore nameplate would be dropped.

It was obviously a blow to Triple Eight. We were the Holden factory-backed outfit in the series, which consisted of 16 Holden Commodores in 2020. The writing had been on the wall, but the shock of the announcement coming on the eve of the new season threw everyone a curveball.

In many ways, it was like knowing someone was critically ill yet it's still a shock when they pass away. We knew Holden was dying, but we were still caught by surprise when it went down.

It was fitting that we delivered the perfect thank-you to Holden by winning the first race of the season. We led from pole position to win my 11th Adelaide podium, defeating McLaughlin by five seconds.

'I want to dedicate this win to Holden,' I proudly declared at the press conference afterwards. 'It has been a bloody tough week for everyone involved. It's great to get a win.

'We got smoked by the other brand here last year, so it is nice to bounce back.'

My hometown of Melbourne was next, with the Supercars round now part of the Formula 1 Australian Grand Prix. It was a great experience to be around the fastest cars in the world.

I'd had the opportunity to drive one back in 2010, through our team sponsor Vodafone. I was able to do four laps of Albert Park, Victoria, in a McLaren Mercedes, which had previously been used by F1 world champion Lewis Hamilton.

This promotion was held on the Wednesday before the Sunday race, and it's still one of the best things I've ever done in my life.

I have this eight-minute movie in my head of those four laps in the F1 car. Let me tell you, it's like being Wile E. Coyote strapped to a rocket trying to chase down the Road Runner. The sheer acceleration is incredible.

While being a racecar driver meant I understood what was going on, things were still happening so fast that in some way it all felt out of control. But I was still holding the throttle flat out, and I managed to get the car up to 307kph down the back straight. I got the data printout afterwards to prove it.

I was so grateful for the experience and to be able to tick that off my bucket list.

However, this visit back to Melbourne wasn't so memorable. After practice and qualifying, the whole event was called off as the growing coronavirus pandemic started to take over our world.

That was the beginning of one of the toughest periods of my professional career, and I wasn't alone in struggling with life under COVID-19 restrictions.

The pandemic threw the whole Supercars calendar out, with events postponed and subsequently cancelled. We didn't race again for more than three months, until the Sydney SuperSprint on 27 June 2020.

We were back there a fortnight later for another two races, as it had become obvious we just had to run the races wherever we could. Over the next three months the Supercars circus moved to Darwin in the Northern Territory, Townsville in Queensland and then down to South Australia.

You were never sure when your next race would be. I described it as like being chased by the invisible boogieman, because we were always on the run from this invisible enemy. You'd get the call to leave Brisbane for the Gold Coast, then suddenly it was North Queensland instead, and then on to Darwin.

It was mentally draining, even though we ended up racing only ten rounds, with the final stop at Bathurst a good summation of my year.

The amount of time on the road had gotten to me. It wasn't the crazy homesickness that I'd experienced previously, but I wasn't myself. I'm naturally a goal-motivated person, but I guess the lack of structure and routine had really thrown me.

While I was still driving flat out and pushing to get the highest possible position, I was also thinking about the end, which is something I'd never done before. Rather than cross the 50-laps-to-go mark and think about maximising the situation, I was thinking I couldn't wait to get to the end of the race. I wasn't slowing down or backing off, I was still pushing it, but the end was in my head. It's like when you go out jogging, you get more out of it if you don't think about the end. And at work, if suddenly the clock hits 5pm and you hadn't really noticed it, those are the best days, rather than when you keep checking the time over and over again.

As soon as you get on the defence in this caper, rather than being offensive-minded, you're in trouble. I was trying to circulate and do a reasonable job, which just wasn't me, and it came back to bite.

Lowndesy did our first stint in the Great Race after we'd qualified in ninth place on the grid, and we'd got up to fifth by lap 33 when I committed the cardinal sin of Bathurst: pushing too hard at the start of a long race.

Everyone says you can't win the race at the start but you can certainly lose it – and I lost it.

It was through the kink before the Cutting, a pair of left-hand corners as you start the climb up the mountain, where I stupidly tried to pass Brodie Kostecki around the outside. He'd been slow out of Griffin's Bend, so I went narrow to try to overtake the Penrite Racing Holden.

The problem was I went too wide, about a car-and-a-half off the normal line, and then was too slow to cut back in front of him when I clearly had the space. I didn't know I had the space, as the visibility in these cars in certain circumstances is poor. Instead, I got caught on a dirty part of the track where the tyres couldn't grip, and that was the end of me.

I speared side-on into the concrete wall at 200kph, causing irreparable damage to the No 88 car.

It was so stupid. I didn't have to attempt that move this early in the race. There would've easily been an opening back down Conrod Straight on the next lap, but I wasn't myself. I wasn't on my game. The team had suffered.

I was filthy afterwards, but I wasn't going to offer the normal reaction that many say in this situation: 'Oh well, there's always next year.' I hate that phrase. I feel it's what the losers say. The reality was I couldn't get Bathurst 2020 back; it was gone.

We've had plenty of misfortune at Bathurst previously, where races didn't go our way when we'd been in good positions and were fighting it out for the win. There was no bad luck on this occasion.

In my 17 years of full-time driving in Supercars, that moment was definitely the lowlight of my career.

12

ON MY OWN TERMS

IT was something I aspired to do: I finished my full-time career on my own terms.

At the end of 2020 I sat down with RD and we both agreed that 2021 was going to be my last season, and that he would also be stepping aside as the managing director of the team. We were both ready for the next stage, and I would spend another 12 months looking over his shoulder, learning all the tricks of the trade in the management game.

I was still going to compete in the endurance events, but what made the decision to hang up my full-time driving helmet feel so right was the fact that it was my *own* decision. That's not always the case in professional sports, but I'm thankful I got to make that decision rather than having it made for me.

To be honest, I probably could've kept going. I was still driving well and had finished the abbreviated 2020 season in fourth position, with four race wins, so I wasn't exactly falling off the cliff.

In fact, I should've finished second in the championship. I'd been a clear second coming into Bathurst, which is why the crash hurt me so much. Being the best of the rest behind Scott McLaughlin, who was dominating at the time, meant something to me.

The thing was, all throughout my career I had never thought about coming second. I was always pushing for the championship. In the penultimate round at South Australia's Tailem Bend in 2020, I could've easily just circled around behind McLaughlin, finished first and second, to hand him the title and secure second place for me. But that wasn't in my DNA. Instead, I lunged at him on the opening lap, which ended with both of us off the track and the stewards hitting me with a 15-second penalty.

The main reason I decided not to continue was because I'd always said I didn't want to hold up a seat, and we're talking about the best seat in the category, from a young kid who was ready to come in and showcase the talents of the next generation.

I'm not greedy. I had 17 years of being a full-time professional racecar driver, and I wanted a young person to have the experiences that I'd had over this journey.

One of the driving forces making sure I was ready for retirement was this paranoia I'd been feeling about being a one-skill wonder.

I started racing when I was seven years old and have basically spent most of my time since then devoted to that pursuit.

Obviously I'm known for being a racecar driver, and one of the best in Australia, which means there is a fair chance my second chapter in life may not be as successful.

That is not going to stop me from doing everything I possibly can to learn multiple skills and be recognised in those fields.

'Recognised' might be the wrong word, because it sounds like I care about what other people think. Recognition isn't what drives me. It's my own personal desire to know that I've done something at a really high standard. I want to get to the end of my life knowing that I've excelled in other areas.

Business management is my next challenge, with my new Triple Eight role and the budding carwash empire, which now has a second outlet in Brisbane with plans to go national.

Filling RD's shoes is going to be tough, and the challenge is going to be to keep the old-school mentality but adapt it to new ways. People like RD have so much experience, and you can't buy experience.

If I can keep those core old-school things that RD does extremely well and then throw in a new mix and modernise some things, then I'll be heading in the right direction.

I've learnt a lot from motor racing and being a professional athlete for so many years. I don't want to waste all of that knowledge and let it go by the wayside. I want to teach up and coming racecar drivers and share all my IP with the next generation.

I am fully aware other athletes have been overconfident about expecting to run a business with the same success they had with their sporting career. It's going to take time for me to learn and adapt, but I don't feel like my ambition is ahead of my ability.

I did manage to sneak another win – the 123rd of my career – at Symmons Plains in April and upstaged my team-mate Shane van Gisbergen, who'd been the dominant force through the start of the 2021 season, winning the opening six races.

Whatever happens on and off the track, my aim is to make the future better, just like my dad always managed to do.

He was a thinker and never took shortcuts, which I found out recently at our cabin on the Murray River. Dad had built a table, which was at the front of our cabin, just beside the water.

He'd built this table with a barbecue inset around this massive gum tree. Every now and then we had to trim it back because as the tree grew it expanded. The frame of the table was in danger of breaking.

Last Christmas I realised I was going to have to redo the whole frame because the tree was getting too big. When I looked underneath the table I found that Dad had actually bolted part of it in, but what was remarkable was he'd also put in new bolt holes for when the tree expanded.

He'd predicted that years down the track the tree was going to grow and this bar, which was the key to the whole table, was going to have to be moved.

It made me smile and appreciate how he used to think and work. He was always about the long game and about making the future better.

I hope I can be the same.

CAREER STATISTICS

JAMIE WHINCUP: SEASON-BY-SEASON SUPERCARS STATISTICS

Year	Starts	Wins	Win %	Podiums	Poles	Rank
2002	2	0	–	0	0	63rd
2003	22	0	–	0	0	27th
2004	2	0	–	0	0	50th
2005	30	0	–	2	0	16th
2006	32	2	6.3%	5	0	10th
2007	37	5	13.5%	20	1	2nd
2008	34	15	44.1%	23	4	1st
2009	26	11	42.3%	15	6	1st
2010	26	9	34.6%	14	9	2nd
2011	28	10	35.7%	19	9	1st
2012	30	12	40.0%	24	7	1st
2013	36	11	30.6%	21	13	1st
2014	38	14	36.8%	21	10	1st
2015	36	8	22.2%	15	6	5th
2016	29	7	24.1%	17	5	2nd
2017	26	4	15.4%	15	2	1st
2018	30	5	16.7%	15	5	3rd
2019	31	5	16.1%	12	2	3rd
2020	27	4	14.8%	14	5	4th

ACKNOWLEDGEMENTS

THINKING of my professional career, there are literally thousands of people who have played a part in my development. There is always a risk when you start naming individuals that you may miss some – in fact, the probability is I most likely will. But, once again, I can't let this fear slow me down.

For many of us, our mum and dad are the most important element in making us who we are, but for me there was the added element of how much time and effort they dedicated to my life. This is a debt I will never be able to repay, but I can certainly try by investing in the next generation.

I had a competitor's father once say to me, 'You have an unfair advantage – you basically have two dads.' In some way, he was right. My uncle Graeme chose not to have children, and he and his partner, Tina, have been as close as a second mum and dad.

Like many, I hated my sister Sally during my teenage years. I know hate is a powerful word, but it felt real. How dare she buzz the front seat of the car every trip to school! ☺ These days I really cherish the time we spend together with Benno and the kids, Mitchell and Chelsea.

Who knows where I would've been and what I would've done without my brothers in crime, Will Davison and Paul Dumbrell. One thing I *do* know is that I'd have a hell of a lot more brain cells! Thanks, fellas.

During my karting days there was a guy by the name of Grant Lindstrom who really had my back in my rookie years and showed us how to go-kart. In the later years, there were Remo Luciani and Peter 'Topsi' Temopoulos, who really cared for me personally. Topsi, in particular, dedicated so much of his own time and shared the wave with me, trying to win the championship. I will never forget not remembering to thank him at an awards night; it still hurts when I think about it, but I've never claimed to be a public speaker.

Roll on, Formula Ford – there was a couple of blokes, Greg Ritter and Sam Astuti, with whom I spent many a weekend away together racing. Good times were had.

As I've mentioned in this book, though, Mick Ritter and my mechanic at the time, Andrew Gilbert, took me from a loose go-kart kid to someone who a respected figure like Garry Rogers would consider worthy of looking after his $600,000 racecar.

Garry, you've been given a bit of stick over the years for getting rid of me, and sorry for sitting back and running with it and using it as a motivator, but you have the thickest skin of anyone I know. Like half the Supercars grid, I can't thank you enough for the opportunity.

Kevin Murphy and a good family friend of mine, Ron Harrop, dragged me back from the dead. Without them, I never would've won a race and experienced the things I have. There is absolutely no shortage of appreciation, I can assure you.

Then we come to my Triple Eight family. As I said in the start, it's dangerous to single anyone out, but I have to. RD, Dutto, Cauchi, Tybo – what a journey! Half my life we've invested together doing what we love most: going racing. Although he's not at Triple Eight anymore and left to go to the dark side, I do have to mention Ludo Lacroix. As a young kid moving out of home and interstate, he treated me like a son.

Moving out of home and interstate felt big at the time, but having my now partner Samantha Watts, who is currently pregnant with our first child, on the journey with me for the last 9 years has made it some of the best years of my life.

There's a bloke who gets around Sanctuary Cove looking like he's just had four Red Bulls and a coffee, but he's actually had neither – his name is Paul Haines. Thanks for pushing me, mate, and for being there when I was in that dark place of *I can't make the finish, it's too hot and I just want to die!* But on top of that, thanks for the laughs.

There have been so many incredible brands I've been more than proud to represent, and look forward to representing well into the future. Most of these brands have meant close relationships with the people associated with them, who have become lifelong friends, which when all is said and done is all that matters. I would love to mention each and every one of you, but it'll end up being an environmental disaster with the paper used!

Finally, my thanks to the beloved fans who have shared this rollercoaster with me. For years now I've always asked myself, *Why me, I don't deserve the dedication and respect.* It's important for you to know, every 50–50 dive, every lap that didn't quite go right, every penalty in the stewards' box, that was for you. Oh, and now that I think of it, there was a bit of champagne shared along the way as well. Yewww!

The scary thing is, I feel like chapter three is about to start, and we're only just getting started.

Let's do this!